HEART OF THE MATTER

letters to my children

HEART OF THE MATTER
Published by Focus Press, Inc.

© Copyright 2011 Focus Press, Inc.
International Standard Book Number 978-0-9829595-3-4
Cover by: Nick Long
Interior design by: Michael Thornton
Cover image by: Thinkstock
Interior images by: Brad and Melinda Harrub

All Scripture quotations are from the New King James Version, copyright
1979, 1980, 1982,
Thomas Nelson, Inc., Publishers, unless otherwise noted.

Printed in the United States of America

For information or to order copies of *Heart of the Matter*,
contact the publisher:

FOCUS PRESS, INC.
1600 WESTGATE CIRCLE, SUITE 125
BRENTWOOD, TN 37027

Library of Congress cataloging-in-publication
Brad Harrub (1970-)
Heart of the Matter
Includes Biblical references
ISBN: 978-0-9829595-3-4
1. Religion. 2. Christian Family. 3. Parenting.
I. Title

HEART OF THE MATTER

letters to my children

By Brad Harrub, Ph.D.

An Open Letter to My Children

Dear Will, Reese, Claire, and Luke,

I want to begin by thanking you for helping me see—even if just in a small way—the love that God has for His children. Your existence on this earth has strengthened my faith, and has caused me on many occasions to take inventory of what is truly important. For a little more than three years I have been working on a project for you. It is what I hope to teach you about many various topics. Some of these you will find funny, and others may even bring a tear to your eye. In many you will find personal reflections that occurred within the house in which you grew up. I hope they make you laugh, but more importantly, I hope they cause you to stop and really think.

While other people may read this book, ultimately it is for you. It is a book of letters that I hope you will read and take to heart. Far too often, I have watched young people who grow up and appear to be faithful Christians, fall prey to the world. This collection of letters is my feeble attempt to make sure you never fall into that category. One of my prayers has been that you see exactly what you read—that the dad who preaches, teaches, and writes, is the same dad who kisses your scrapes and scares away the monsters at night.

I hope you will read this book several times, at different points in your life. I think it will mean different things for you at different times. For instance, once you have left our home and found a mate you might find some new nuggets that you had not seen before. If God blesses you with children, I think you will find even more nuggets hidden within my letters. Keep it handy, and don't be afraid to pass it along to your children.

I don't have to tell you all that I am not a perfect dad. There are many things in life I didn't get right. I'm not a phenomenal basketball player, and I can't fix everything that breaks around our house. Even when it comes to how I trained each one of you, I often found myself falling short. Your mom and I were constantly re-evaluating our parenting methods and expectations. But one thing I do know—God's Word is perfect. And it holds the perfect prescription for everything that you will confront during your lifetime.

You all know that your dad goes out most weekends to teach about God and His Word. While I love my job and am passionate about teaching the Truth, there is nothing more important to me than the eternal destiny of **your** souls. My existence revolves around making sure our family gets to heaven. I pray that each one of you not only knows that, but that you also realize I will do whatever is necessary to strengthen your walk with Christ. We have talked on occasion about the sacrifices you have to make for me to be able to do that. I appreciate your willingness to join me in our family vision. My prayer is that you will read this book and it will remind you of that vision.

From a very young age I have tried to teach you two main goals in life (and I know that if I asked you could recite them):
Goal #1—Get to Heaven.
Goal #2—Take as many people with you as you possibly can.

I'm begging you to never forget those goals. Never allow them to take a backseat to something else. Never compromise Him or His Word.

Heart of the Matter

Some people mark their success by measures of wealth, fame, or position. This is a common practice in our secular society. I will view myself as a success—if, and only if—I hear God tell each one of you, "Well done thy good and faithful servant, ... enter into the joy of the Lord." It will be at that moment that I will smile and realize that I was a successful man.

One final word before you begin. That "success" will not be mine alone. You will never know how much your mother loves each one of you, and how much of her life she has devoted to getting each of you to Heaven. I have watched her give, and give, and give— and just when I thought she had nothing left to give, she opens up her heart even wider and blesses our family with more love. In most cases she deserves all of the credit. I'll claim the mistakes, she gets credit for the accomplishments. She is a remarkable woman and you are blessed to be able to call her Mom. I hope as your relationship with her matures that you will lean on her for wisdom. I pray that you will use her as an invaluable resource when you have your own children. I hope the Lord blesses me with enough health to watch your relationship with her "evolve" from one of parent-child into friend-friend.

Again, I thank you for changing my life and giving me the opportunity to love each one of you. I pray God will rain down His richest blessings on each of you, and that you will all serve as warriors for Him.

With All My Love,

Dad

10. 10

Acknowledgements

My life and my work intersect with hundreds of people who play a vital role in everything I do. This book is really a book that was "written" by you—I just had the pleasure of putting the words to paper. I know I will leave many people out—and for that I would ask your forgiveness! You know who you are, and I am thankful to have you in my life. Special thanks to Chuck Davis and his family who are walking the Christian walk! Check out his awesome web page at www.christiancenteredlessons.com. To Rod and Cindy Wilson, thanks for letting me stay at the cabin. Your hospitality was a much-needed recharge. To Mary Sue Lockwood, your ongoing support continues to amaze me. To the Frazier Park congregation, I made you a promise and I will continue to uphold that promise. Thank you for allowing dreams to come true! To Andy and Katina Gaines (and Anna Claire), thanks for your friendship and believing in our work. To the Wilkie family, thanks for demonstrating much of what is in this book! To Mark Teske, thanks for always having an ear to share with me.

To the Birdwell Lane congregation, you supported me with Convicted and then came back for more! I truly appreciate your generosity and vision.

To my staff—thanks for making our "happy place" such a happy place. You guys are the greatest! I know I ask a tremendous amount from each one of you—and you always come through for me. Thanks for remaining sane even on those occasions when I'm on the road for weeks at a time! And thanks for catching the vision.

To my proofers—Tonja, Bernadine, and Jack. Thanks for making me sound educated and fixing all my misepellings. Any remaining mistakes in this book are because I refused their wise counsel and proceeded blindly in the dark! You guys are the best.

To the readers of *Think* magazine. Thanks for your encouragement and kind words regarding the Heart of the Matter articles.

To my wife I saved the best for last. Thank you for being such an incredible person. Thanks for instilling the words of this book into the hearts of our children. Thank you for being a phenomenal Christian wife, and an exceptional Christian mother. I know you don't believe you deserve to be praised, but your hard work is evident in the four children who call you Mom. I look forward to reading your book one day—because you have so much more wisdom to share. Thank you for being our rock!

Dedication

This book is dedicated to four individuals who taught me a whole new level of love: Will, Reese, Claire, and Luke. I love each one of you. Never forget your #1 goal in life.

Table of Contents

Introduction

"They don't come with a manual." That's the common response we hear when individuals start talking to new parents about their children. What they really mean is you are going to get some things right, and others, you will foul up royally. But the truth is, they do come with a manual, a book that has sage wisdom for every aspect of life—but sadly, a book that for many people has become a reference book that is only opened on Sunday mornings during worship or Bible class.

Let me begin by admitting up front that I am not an expert. If you are looking for a step-by-step proven method on how to raise faithful children, you have come to the wrong place. I am simply a Christian father who is tremendously concerned about the spiritual welfare of my children. My "wisdom" is not of myself, but rather it comes from God's Word. If you share a common concern for your children or grandchildren, then perhaps you have come to the right place.

We can no longer ignore the epidemic that surrounds us. Our children are leaving the church in droves. We've all seen or heard the statistics that more than 75% of our young people walk away from the church, choosing instead to embrace humanism—and a life of instant gratification. We can no longer ignore the massive elephant that is in the room with us. Almost every family has been touched by the pain of having a relative abandon his or her spiritual foundation. We must shake ourselves awake from the apathetic stupor that has held previous generations.

I am convinced that if we are going to make changes—changes in the statistics, changes in morality, changes in politics, changes in church leadership, and changes in marriage and family—those changes must start in the home. The old adage about the hand that rocks the cradle rules the world has some extremely strong truths. If we are going to change things, we must make some fundamental changes in the home. We must reclaim our children and build a hedge of protection around them, all the while teaching them the Truths found in His Word.

The cold hard truth is that what you will read in this book does not come easy and it requires time. Many people want "results," but they are unwilling to put in the time. If I were looking you in the eye right now, I would ask you two questions at this point: (1) Are you willing to put your children's spiritual welfare ahead of everything else in life? (2) Are you actually willing to put in the time and energy required to make it happen? Faithful children do not happen by mistake or accident. They are the product of deliberate parenting.

Please understand that much of what you read in the following pages is contrary to everything the world is telling you. I hope that in some small way this book will challenge you to redefine "normal." It's time Christians cast off the shackles that say that we must fit into some mold the world has constructed for us. It is time we believe and act like New Testament Christians.

The reason for this book is simple. For a decade I have listened to Christian parents who, through tear-filled eyes, have shared story after story of how their children grew up in the church but have now gone off into the world. While there is not a common reason or thread that ties all of these stories together, it is very apparent that many of these young people were hearing one thing from the pulpit and hearing (through actions and words) a totally different message the rest of the week. They heard from the pulpit that we should abstain from immorality, and then sat down with Mom and Dad and watched the latest episode of "Desperate House-wives". Or they heard about creation but then ran off to school, only to be indoctrinated with the evolutionary theory.

Many of the children who have walked away from the church can provide correct Bible answers to various questions—but those facts never reached their hearts. They learned factoids, but those factoids never altered the essence of who they are or Whose they are.

These are letters to my children. Within these real letters is what I hope to teach my four children. But understand that I am not a perfect or an all-knowing father. My children are not perfect as well, and I don't expect perfection from them. But I do pray for and expect faithfulness to God from each one of them. Notice I said "expect" and not "hope." It is time Christians raise the bar and stop "hoping" our children will turn out faithful. Hope is not a strategy for success. It is time we act. It is time we get down and discuss the **heart of the matter.**

bh

Having looked in the tearful eyes of many parents whose children have abandoned the Faith, I have learned there are a million miles between our children "going through the motions" in reference to their spiritual lives versus our children possessing hearts that dictate their actions. In this book, I plan to share with you what I hope to instill in the hearts of my children and those whom I love.

Letters ...
Regarding Church Life

Your Relationship With God

The vast majority of people in the United States say they believe in God—but their actions say otherwise. Likewise, those who profess to be Christians recognize that the greatest command is to love God with all of our hearts, souls, and minds (Matthew 22:37), and yet, very few demonstrate that kind of love for God. Rarely does our "love" for God translate into action. Most Christians are comfortable and will continue to worship and sing praises to God, as long as they don't have to make large sacrifices. We will meet for an hour or two a week, but we are not going to actually give up many of the worldly activities or niceties of life we enjoy. Consider just how much would actually change in many people's lives if they no longer "loved" God. Would anything really change? They would still watch the same television shows, participate in the same activities, and wear the same clothes. This is not the love Jesus commanded.

This lukewarm love (Acts 3:16) has poisoned the church. In America we have created an environment where God is worshipped in luxurious buildings and we "hire out" our benevolence and evangelism. We have Americanized and sanitized the Gospel so that no one has to get his hands dirty or give up anything. As a result, many hearts have forgotten their first love. The words Jesus quoted from Isaiah should ring in our ears, "These people draw near to Me with their mouth, and honor Me with their lips, but their heart is far from Me" (Matthew 15:8). We say we love God but we refuse to turn our lives over to Him as we continue to be a slave to the god of "control." We love God primarily because we feel we should and not because of genuine love that pours deeply out of our hearts. And our children can see it—or rather a lack of it. I think in many Bible classes we learn His precepts and we learn doctrine, but we never teach our children how to establish a relationship with Him.

Here is what I intend to teach my children about loving God.

I've been purposefully waiting to write this letter, as it hits close to home, and it is extremely important. There is a massive difference between saying you believe in God versus actually forming a relationship with Him. I am earnestly praying that you will develop that relationship with God—a love that supersedes everything else in this life. Look at Psalm 63:1-5 and meditate on the picture David paints. This sincere love was something that I sadly did not learn until fairly recently. Allow me to try to describe just what I'm talking about.

When your mom and I were dating and engaged, my world revolved around the next time I would get to see her. I worked evenings and nights at the hospital, so oftentimes we had to be creative about when we could get together. For instance, we might have a picnic at midnight instead of during the day. Or we might see one another very early in the morning if I worked the night shift. I would go to great lengths to tell her of my love for her (get her to tell you about the signs along the road). I knew she liked chocolate, so I would surprise her weekly with chocolates, flowers, and gifts. We would talk on the phone until the wee hours of the morning. Hours spent apart were often spent thinking about when we would be together again. I would literally do anything (within the sphere of Christianity) for her. I was (and still am!) madly in love with your mom. My sincere love caused (and causes) me to act on my feelings.

That is what I pray you will have for God—a love that causes you to want to be with Him more than anything else. Focus your attention on the greatest command: "You shall love the Lord your God with all your heart, with all your soul, and with all your mind" (Matthew 22:37). I pray your world revolves around Him and your time with Him. Don't allow individuals to Americanize this verse to say, "Love God with all your heart, soul, and mind if it is convenient and does not require too many sacrifices." Seek a love that will actually change the way you live and cause you to "go upstream" against the apathy we find in many churches today. Some individuals will think that this is radical and may feel uncomfortable with the thought of it—as it may expose an absence of love for God in their own lives. But I pray that your love for God causes you to turn this world upside down (Acts 17:6)!

Let me freely admit I don't have all of the answers on how to build this love, as it is an ongoing part of my life. I think in order to establish this type of relationship you need to start concentrating more on eternity and less on life on earth. Not a day should pass by without you considering Heaven and the fact that this could be the day you meet Jesus! Our love for God should start when we honestly comprehend the magnitude of who God really is (Isaiah 42:5). If you spend time each day really considering the creative power of God (Psalm 19) and what the Lord has done, your love for Him will grow. How could it not grow when you really consider His creation! I suspect you will find yourself praising God more readily.

Too often individuals look around, and, instead of seeing the majesty and awesomeness of God, they see what they don't have.

Set aside some time to meditate on the holiness of God (Isaiah 6:3; Revelation 4:8). By focusing on who God is, it will become apparent that He cannot have anything to do with sin and still be God. It is virtually impossible to be running the race and pursue God and sin at the same time. Normally you have to stop one to do the other. Focusing on God will help you run toward Him and leave you less time for sin and trouble. Finally, take time each day to focus on God's love toward man (John 3:16), and the fact that Jesus conquered death. No matter what comes at you in this life it pales in comparison to the fact that we can have eternal life with Him. If you do this daily, I believe it will prevent what one author deemed "spiritual amnesia."

Notice that these focal points have absolutely nothing to do with you, and everything to do with God. Most people are living their lives as though "it's all about me," when the harsh reality is they are just a speck of sand among many in a galaxy too big to fully comprehend. When you begin to focus on God rather than self, your life will soon reflect it. With these eternal thoughts come the realization that many are spiritually dead, and the urgency to teach them about God. That's where our love for God can call us to action.

Some individuals would encourage you to blindly follow the pathway society has set before you and "wait" for God to reveal His plan for you. They find comfort in "waiting" for God. One wonders if these same individuals "wait" to go sporting events, to go on vacation, or to play golf. I suspect their love of these secular things cause them to act! True love will freely bring about sacrifice and action (1 John 3:16-20). Many of these same individuals are living under the false impression that if they live good lives and are kind, then lost souls will come up and want to know about Jesus. Wrong! Consider for a moment the fact that there are "good"

22

and "kind" lost souls who don't know Jesus. Are people coming up to them as well? Your love for God should cause you to get outside of your comfort zone and tell others about Him.

Real relationships take work and effort. Cultivate the relationship. Spend time with Him. And above all else, love Him with all of your heart!

Love,

Dad

"My son, keep your father's command, And do not forsake the law of your mother"
- Proverbs 6:20

No More Excuses

As a parent and teacher, I am acutely aware of the questions that many pose as a means to absolve themselves from any responsibility toward God. "What about the poor innocent Aborigines in Australia? Is God really going to send the 'poor innocent Aborigine' to Hell—even though they have never heard the Good News of Jesus Christ? Furthermore, is He really going to send millions of 'innocent' people to Hell just because they have not obeyed the Gospel?" While I won't judge the motives of the individual asking the question, I am inclined to believe that this question is often used as a deflection or an escape tactic by those who do not want to humble themselves before Almighty God.

Here is what I intend to teach my children regarding lost souls:

First, I have never met a "poor innocent Aborigine" from Australia or any other country. The key word there is *innocent*. Innocence would indicate this person has never sinned and is therefore not in need of the cleansing blood of Jesus Christ. The Bible clearly indicates that , "all have sinned and fall short of the glory of God" (Romans 3:23; cf. 1 John 1:8-10). So we can safely know that every person of an accountable age on this planet has at some point sinned—an act that separates us from God (Isaiah 59:2).

Second, the sad facts are that there are people on this planet who have never heard the Gospel. While the Bible indicates that all men in times past heard the Good News (Colossians 1:23; Matthew 24:14), we know today that many generations have passed since that declaration. Sadly, the population has been steadily increasing while the zeal and evangelistic efforts of many Christians have been steadily decreasing. (As we discussed in the October 2007 issue of Think, one of the problems facing Christians today is apathy—something for which we will stand in judgment).

So what then of the poor "sinful" Aborigine? Do they get a free pass to Heaven? Absolutely not! The inspired Word of God indicates that sin separates us from God, and therefore they too are separated. But what about that word "innocent"? Are they truly innocent? Could ancient tribes of Indians, or children reared in a predominately Hindu culture grow up on this planet and never see evidence of a Supreme Being? In other words, can someone know God exists without being taught? Again, I believe the Bible addresses this as well.

In Romans 1:18-20, Paul is discussing the wrath of God on those who are unrighteous. In verses 19-20, he wrote, "Because what may be known of God is manifest in them, for God has shown **it** to them. For since the creation of the world His invisible **attributes** are clearly seen, being understood by the things that are made, **even** His eternal power and Godhead, so that they are without excuse" (emp. added). Paul was telling those Christians in Rome that God's invisible attributes have been clearly seen since the Creation of the world. He then stresses that even His eternal power and Godhead can be understood. But notice the last phrase: "So that they are without excuse."

While many people living in America today are counting on playing the "ignorance" card on the Day of Judgment, Paul tells us that it is not going to work! It's not enough to say to God, "If only I had known. If only You had given me a sign." Paul is revealing that those signs have been around literally since Creation! Paul, in essence, has stripped away the excuse that millions of people are counting on for that Great Day.

This truth does not give me any pleasure, and it certainly does not rest easy on my mind. In fact, I believe it places a tremendous burden on those of us who know the Truth. Since my children were little, I have taught them that their number one goal in life (above everything else) is to get to Heaven. The second goal in life that I am trying to instill in my children is that we are to take as many people as we can with us to Heaven. **Only when we realize just how many individuals around us are in a lost condition will the importance of this goal be fully comprehended**.

As further evidence that God can be known, the inspired Psalmist observed, "The heavens declare the glory of God; and the firmament shows His handiwork" (Psalm 19:1). The implication is that the existence of God can be known through His creation.

I think it is important that we recognize that prior to the birth of Jesus that millions of people were guilty of rejecting God—not Christ, because He was not here yet. Thus, several generations of people were judged guilty by God not for rejecting Christ, but for rejecting Him. God expected these people to come to know Him and ultimately obey Him. Where does this judgment leave those "Aborigines" who are also rejecting Him today?

From these simple points, we can know that all humans have sinned and that our iniquities have separated us from God. We can further know that the existence and power of God can be known simply through His creation. Yes, many people (like the militant atheists of today) will suppress that truth, but this does not negate the fact. Now back to the individual living in the back-country of some third world country, or the millions who have not obeyed the Truth. What is their fate? Is it hopeless for them?

Again, we must turn to God's Word. In Deuteronomy 4:29 Moses wrote, "But from there you will seek the Lord your God, and you will find Him if you seek Him with all of your heart and with all of your soul." This proclamation is confirmed in Jeremiah 29:13, "And you will seek Me and find Me, when you search for Me with all your heart."

Clearly, the text indicates that if one truly seeks God, then he or she **will** find Him. I firmly believe that this is where faithful Christians must zealously step into the picture. Through actions (funding and sending missionaries to other countries), through print (magazines, tracts, study courses), through media (internet, radio, and television), we must be there for those who are seeking.

The heart of the matter is that there are no innocent people on the planet. Sin separates people from the Creator. However, God

can be known, and those who **seek** Him **will find** Him. How will these truths affect your daily actions?

Love,

Dad

"My son, give attention to my words; Incline your ear to my sayings,"
- Proverbs 4:20

Yes We Get To

We've all said it before, sometimes without ever considering the underlying message: "Get ready, we have to go to…." The words "have to" oftentimes send a message to our children that this may not be something we "want to" (or get to) do. Not too many children would ever say "We **have to** go to an amusement park." Their joy and desire would change their demeanor and language to exclaim, "We **get to** go to an amusement park!" Our attitude and vocabulary are extremely influential in how young people view things. So what is the verbiage we use when we discuss the Church, prayer, worship, mission works, giving, singing, and even Heaven? Is it something we "have to" do, or do we remind our children that these are things we "get to" do?

Here is what I intend to teach my children about "having to" versus "getting to" and the power of attitude.

Unfortunately, there will always be things in life that we don't look forward to, but we still "have to" do them. For instance, I have to clean out the garage, or my car won't fit! I have to take out the garbage on Sunday nights, because our pickup day is Monday. But when it comes to Christianity and serving our God, these are things we should want to do—things we look forward to. That's why on Sunday morning you hear your mom and I say, "Get ready, we get to go to Church today." Or why before we eat we will often remind you "we get to pray" instead of "we have to pray".

Anytime you begin to approach your Christianity with a feeling of "have to," I want you to stop and remind yourself who you are and Who God is (Psalm 46:10). Spend a few minutes in the Psalms to help refresh your memory of the power of our Creator (e.g., Psalm 19). David wrote, "When I consider Your heavens, the work of Your fingers, the moon and the stars, which You have ordained, **what is man that You are mindful of him,** and the son of man that You visit him?" (Psalm 8:3-4, emp. added). When we approach the Church with an attitude of "have to" then it tells me we have forgotten Who God is, how powerful He is, and ultimately what He did for us. How can anyone read John 3:16 and consider attending worship something we "have to" do?

The temptation may arise during your life in which you view your life as important or too busy — and thus church is one more thing you have to fit into your schedule. But remember, without God you would have no life or schedule to fill. Never view worship or spiritual matters with "have to" attitude. Joyfully make the time to praise His name and thank Him for all your blessings.

Throughout God's Word, we see people with both the "have to" and "get to" attitudes. Consider the difference in Jonah's life if he had viewed God's initial request to go to Nineveh as a "get to" opportunity (Jonah1:1-17). Do you think Paul viewed going to Macedonia as something he "had to" do? The text says, "Now after he saw the vision, immediately we sought to go to Macedonia, concluding that the Lord had called us to preach the gospel to them" (Acts 16:9-10). Do you think those who were convicted in their hearts on the day of Pentecost (Acts 2:37-41) were thinking, "Oh man, now I have to get baptized to have my sins washed away?" Or rather, did they gladly receive the Word and were baptized?

Before you were born, your mother and I had the opportunity to do some mission work overseas. On one occasion, the building that we were supposed to hold a meeting in had been chained and locked by local authorities and local orthodox priests. But that didn't stop those in the area who wanted to hear the Truth. These people possessed a deep "want to/get to" attitude toward God and His Word. Do not let the cares of this world affect your attitude toward God and His Church. When it comes to giving, mission work, worship, singing, praying, and ultimately getting to Heaven, these should be things we look forward to—things we want to do.

Lionel Richie sings a song titled "Easy Like Sunday Morning." In a few years you may have children running around the house and you will realize the falsehood (and utter ridiculousness!) of this song. Many Sunday mornings are downright hectic and crazy as we search for the right socks or bows. But I pray if you ever find yourself telling your own children, "Come on, we have to go to church," that you will stop and remember this simple lesson on the power of your attitude.

Love,

Dad

"A wise man will hear and increase learning, And a man of understanding will attain wise counsel,"
- Proverbs 1:5

Don't Check Your Brain at the Door

Most of us have felt that feeling when we are tired, concerned, or stressed that, while we may be present "physically," we are not there mentally. I suspect most of us have even said something in the past like: "I'm here physically, but not mentally." But what happens when this attitude infects our worship? How many times have Christians entered an auditorium for worship, only to check their brains at the door? It is no secret that individuals today can sing and take part in the Lord's Supper but be mentally absent from worshipping God. Internally we may be focusing on someone's new hairstyle, the preacher's clothes, where to eat lunch, or an upcoming ball game. Yes, we are physically in worship, but our attitudes demonstrate that we never acknowledge being in the presence of Jehovah God. Sadly, there are occasions when people are worried about critiquing the preacher, the roast in the crockpot, passing notes, whispering, personal grooming, playing with children, etc., and thus, they never mentally engage for worship.

Here is what I intend to teach my children about mentally engaging for worship.

The mainstream media has done an incredible job of painting Christians with a broad-brush as ignorant individuals. Hollywood has reconfirmed this label by frequently showing Christians as weak-minded and foolish people who don't have enough strength to cope with life on their own. Sadly, this label is occasionally well warranted. There are times in which Christians don't use their God-given brains—and they never truly engage their minds during worship. Do not fall into this temptation—no matter how much is going on in your life. **Take a few moments to clear your thoughts and remind yourself why you are doing what you are doing and Who the ultimate audience is for our worship.**

Consider one example in which the Lord observed: "Inasmuch as these people draw near with their mouths and honor Me with their lips, but have removed their hearts far from Me, and their fear toward Me is taught by the commandment of men…" (Isaiah 29:13). We know from the text that the people had offered their sacrifices (Isaiah 1:11ff), but their attitude was one of just going through the motions. Jesus used this very passage to rebuke the Pharisees: "Hypocrites! Well did Isaiah prophesy about you, saying: 'These people draw near to Me with their mouth, And honor Me with their lips, But their heart is far from Me. And in vain they worship Me, teaching as doctrines the commandments of men'" (Matthew 15:7-9). These were people who were going through the motions, but their hearts were not in it.

On another occasion, Jesus again commented on attitude, rebuking the Pharisees saying: "Woe to you, scribes and Pharisees, hypocrites! For you pay tithe of mint and anise and cummin, and have neglected the weightier matters of the law: justice and mercy and faith. These you ought to have done, without leaving the others undone" (Matthew 23:23). The Pharisees were correctly observing some of the small details of worship, but they completely neglected why they were doing what they were doing. Their hearts (and minds) were in the wrong place. They weren't mentally engaged in what they were doing.

Never forget that the fear of the Lord is the beginning of wisdom (Psalm 111:10; Proverbs 1:7).

In Paul's admonitions to Timothy he told him, "**Study** to shew thyself approved unto God, a workman that needeth not to be ashamed, rightly dividing the word of truth" (2 Timothy 2:15 KJV, emp. added). God has not called us to be unintelligent. Rather, He wants us to study and be able to defend His Word. In 1 Thessalonians 5:21, we are commanded to "Test all things; hold fast what is good." In James 1:5 we read, "If any of you lacks wisdom, let him ask of God, who gives to all liberally and without reproach, and it will be given to him." Do these admonitions sound like crutches for weak-minded people? Christianity is a religion based on evidence and intelligence. Don't forget that!

Love,

Dad

"The name of the Lord is a strong tower; The righteous run to it and are safe."
- Proverbs 18:10

A Bloody Mess

Worship settings today are relatively clean. Many auditoriums are fully carpeted with padded pews and air-conditioning. Flowers decorate the front of the auditorium as polished preachers, dressed in formal attire, stand behind large podiums. On any given Sunday, New Testament Christians can be seen wearing their finest clothing as they lift their voices in song to God. However, this "sterile" environment has caused many Christians to forget about the necessity of blood in our worship. I think many have forgotten blood is required for the remission of sins. The writer of Hebrews noted, "And according to the law almost all things are purified with blood, and without shedding of blood there is no remission" (Hebrews 9:22).

Here is what I intend to teach my children about blood and sacrifices.

From a young age, your dad was always intrigued by blood. During your lifetime, you will encounter many people who get queasy (or even faint) at the mere sight of it. For some reason, I was always drawn to it. Working in the emergency department, I witnessed firsthand more than my fair share. I can still immediately recognize the unique smell of iron-rich blood. The blood that has always held my interest is also a key component to the forgiveness of sins.

Approximately 4000 years ago, God took the Israelites out of Egypt and organized a priestly form of worship that was strongly dependent on animal sacrifices. Blood became a very real and a very prominent reminder of their obedience to God. We learn there were voluntary offerings (burnt offerings, meal offerings, and peace offerings) in which animals were bled and burned (Leviticus 7:12-18). There were also compulsory cleansing offerings (sin offerings and guilt offerings) that involved the blood and sacrifice of animals (Leviticus 4:1-6:7).

In order to truly appreciate the importance of this blood, consider what God said to Moses: "For the life of the flesh is in the blood, and I have given it to you upon the altar to make atonement for your souls; for it is the blood that makes atonement for the soul" (Leviticus 17:11). In the prior chapter, we learn that part of the Day of Atonement required Aaron to "take some of the blood of the bull and some of the blood of the goat, and put it on the horns of the altar all around" (16:18). This helps explain one of the major differences we see between the Tabernacle (or Temple) and our modern auditoriums. Unlike modern church buildings, the tabernacle was fashioned for offering daily sacrifices to God in order to keep this nation clean and acceptable to God. Think of it as a butchering and burning place rather than a room full of pews. Animals were routinely killed, cut up, and burned in an effort to make the Israelites clean. Blood was a part of how they presented themselves worthy of God's presence.

However, the blood could not completely eradicate sins. We learn in Hebrews 11:4, "It is not possible that the blood of bulls and goats could take away sins." It would be Christ's crucifixion that eventually nailed the Old Law to the cross (Colossians 2:13-15) and His blood that forgives our sins. "But Christ came as High Priest of the good things to come with the greater and more perfect tabernacle not made with hands, that is, not of this creation. Not with the blood of goats and calves, but with His own blood He entered the Most Holy Place once for all, having obtained eternal redemption" (Hebrews 9:11-12).

When Jesus went to the cross, He became a spotless sacrifice for the sins of mankind.

The Bible describes it as, "The precious blood of Christ, as of a lamb without blemish and without spot" (1 Peter 1:19).

The priestly nation and sacrificial system was abolished with His blood. "And every priest stands ministering daily and offering repeatedly the same sacrifices, which can never take away sins. But this Man, after He had offered one sacrifice for sins forever, sat down at the right hand of God" (Hebrews 10:11-12). Suddenly the need for blood sacrifices disappeared and people could address God directly with Jesus as their mediator. Hopefully, you can see why their form of worship changed dramatically.

We come into contact with the blood of Christ when we are buried in baptism (Romans 6:3-4). It is that blood that is able to continually cleanse us: "But if we walk in the light as He is in the light, we have fellowship with one another, and the blood of Jesus Christ His Son cleanses us from all sin" (1 John 1:7). So the next time you scrape a knee or cut a finger, take a second to consider what His blood did for us—and how special His blood truly is.

Love,

"There is a way that seems right to a man, But its end is the way of death."
- Proverbs 16:25

Death

She lived to be over one hundred, and to this day I can still remember the smell of her perfume, lotion, and the stale smell of tobacco when she kissed my cheek. We called her Granny Morgan, and she was my great-grandmother. She was one of those unforgettable characters who loved life and loved to tell stories. She was also the first person who gave me my first-hand experience with death. I was only seven years old when she died—but those memories linger still.

Anyone who has had the pleasure of walking this Earth for more than a couple of decades has experienced the pain of death. It is the one thing we can all count on. Death is not prejudiced or biased; it affects the rich and poor, black and white, religious and non-believers. Oftentimes death causes so much emotional strain that it can stress our relationship with God. We question why He would allow someone close to us to die.

Here is what I intend to teach my children about death.

Death is part of the circle of life. In Ecclesiastes, we read that there is a time to be born and a time to die (3:2). Death was brought into the world by the sin of Adam and Eve (Genesis 2:17), and has continued ever since (1 Corinthians 15:21). Having spent several years working in a hospital, I have probably witnessed hundreds of people slipping into eternity. It's a very odd thing to talk to someone and then realize in the next minute they are gone. Just think, every year that passes holds the anniversary day of your death. It's one of the few things in the world that money, influence, or fame cannot change—it is inevitable.

But I want to make sure you always keep a proper perspective of death. For you see, death is not something to be scared of or try to avoid. In fact, for those who have obeyed God, death is the beginning of a reward (2 Timothy 4:7-8). In the medical profession, death is often viewed as a failure, but the truth is that for Christians, death is victory. Paul wrote to the Christians in Philippi and declared, "For to me, to live is Christ, and to die is gain" (Philippians 1:21). **Never forget that this loss is ultimately a "gain."** During your lifetime, you will have the opportunity to attend the funerals of individuals who are Christians and those who are not. One of the things I hope you recognize is the difference in the atmosphere—at Christian funerals there is almost a joy in the air, as everyone knows where that person will spend eternity. However, the death of a non-Christian is usually a very solemn and often gut-wrenching occasion. I cannot think of anything worse than having to preach the funeral of someone who is not a Christian—because at that point they no longer have the ability to obey God. Their eternal destiny has already been determined.

You have heard me say many times that if ever I am on a plane that crashes, I would be happy and at peace—because I know I'm "going home" to receive my crown of life (Revelation 2:10). Never forget that as faithful Christians we can know where we will spend eternity (1 John 5:13). My only sadness will be leaving you and your mother, temporarily, while you continue to reside here on the Earth. But that's not "the end."

While death does mean we are separated, we can feel a great deal of comfort during our time of loss. It is my prayer that as you mature you will give a lot more thought to the topic of "eternity" rather than death. Study what the Bible has to say about eternal life—and what is required (e.g., Matthew 18:8; Matthew 19:29; Matthew 25:46) It's hard to even fathom that amount of time. But I look forward to spending it with you and those we love. Never, ever forget your #1 and #2 goals in life. See you there…

Love,

Dad

"If the righteous will be recompensed on the earth, How much more the ungodly and the sinner."
- Proverbs 11:31

Resurrection

Every year thousands of Muslims make a pilgrimage to Mecca to the tomb of Muhammad. Likewise, followers of Confucianism visit the grave of Confucius in Qufu, Shandong Province of China. Similarly, the Temple of the Tooth or "Dalada Maligawa" is believed to house some of the cremated ashes of Buddha. Having been buried centuries ago, the physical bodies of these religious founders are slowly turning to dust as millions journey to pay honor and respect.

Christianity is unique in that we serve a risen Savior. There are no remains to which to pilgrimage. Our Savior Jesus Christ fully conquered death. For those skeptics who vehemently cling to naturalistic causes for everything, the bodily resurrection of Jesus seems ludicrous. They laugh at the very notion. Yet, what does the evidence prove?

Here is what I intend to teach my children about the resurrection.

Everything hinges on the resurrection of Jesus Christ. Paul wrote to the church in Corinth, "And if Christ is not risen, then our preaching is empty and your faith is also empty. Yes, and we are found false witnesses of God, because we have testified of God that He raised up Christ, whom He did not raise up—if in fact the dead do not rise. For if the dead do not rise, then Christ is not risen. And if Christ is not risen your faith is futile; you are still in your sins" (1 Corinthians 15:14-17). Simply put, if Jesus could not make it out of the tomb, we don't have any hope.

When you consider the resurrection, ask yourself first and foremost: **Who moved the stone?** Make no doubt about it: the individuals living at that time took ample measure to make sure the tomb was secure. The chief priests and Pharisees spoke to Pilate and said, "Sir we remember while He was still alive, how that deceiver said 'After three days I will rise.' Therefore command that the tomb be made secure until the third day, lest His disciples come by night and steal Him away" (Matthew 27:63-64). We learn from Matthew's account that the stone in front of the tomb was sealed and a guard was assigned to watch the tomb (27:65-66).

And yet, even with all of this preparation, the tomb was found empty. Logic tells us that if the Jews took the body, they would have paraded it all around town denouncing the notion that Jesus was indeed the Messiah. If they really knew where the body was, it would have surfaced not long after the crucifixion. Likewise, if the disciples took the body then they would have known for certain that the resurrection was a hoax. Not only did they preach about the bodily resurrection of Jesus, but many also went to their deaths in proclaiming it. Who would go to his own death perpetuating a lie? A stranger off the street would not have taken it for fear of the guard and breaking the seal—besides what use would the body have been to a stranger? None of these options is logical—and yet the tomb remains empty.

I have come to regard the resurrection as probably the best "Christian evidence" material in existence. Scholars who don't believe in the Bible will concede that a man named Jesus walked the earth and was crucified. We have ancient historical writings that serve as evidence for these events. But how can one explain away the empty tomb? Again, who rolled away the stone? How was it that Saul—who would later become the apostle Paul—was so utterly convinced of the resurrection? Additionally, why would thousands of religious people change their day of worship from the Sabbath (Saturday–Exodus 20:8, Exodus 31:15-19) to the first day of the week (Sunday–Acts 6:7; 21:20)? Finally, why would thousands of Jews be pricked in their hearts on the day of Pentecost (Acts 2) if it were merely a hoax?

Jesus conquered death.

This exciting fact gives meaning to every aspect of our modern-day worship. We now have a mediator through which we can pray. It gives meaning to the Lord's Supper that we observe on the first day of the week. The truth that Jesus came out of the grave gives Christians the hope that we too will one day spend eternity with Him! Study the resurrection, for it will certainly strengthen your faith.

Love,

*"One who turns away
his ear from hearing the
law, Even his prayer is an
abomination."
- Proverbs 28:9*

Prayer

How many children reared in Christian homes sit down to eat a meal never giving thought to slowing down to offer a prayer to God and thank Him for the food? Or, how often is the kitchen the only place in the home where prayers are offered? In some homes, these "prayers" are memorized lines that are orated or sung quickly so that everyone can eat.

Every Sunday morning we have the wonderful opportunity to join together during worship and pray to God. Many congregations have set aside specific times (e.g., opening prayer, closing prayer) during their services, which allow members to praise and petition God. This is a special time in which we have to bestow honor to God, to plead for intercessions, to make our supplications known, and to beg for forgiveness. I suspect many of us are guilty for taking our mediator—Jesus Christ—for granted. In 1 Timothy 2:5 we read, "For there is one God and one Mediator between God and men, the Man Christ Jesus." Men of old did not have this mediator, and were not in the blessed position that we find ourselves today.

Sadly, prayer oftentimes becomes a "to-do" item that is carried out with little thought—simply to check it off the list. Words blur together as men repeat the exact same phrases week after week. In fact, many teens can quote a list of "prayerisms" that have been repeated so often that for many they have lost their meaning.

Add to this that many individuals no longer believe in the power of prayer. There are Christians who will participate in prayer, but deep down in their heart-of-hearts they don't believe the prayers of righteous men can avail anything. They ask in "hope," but not

faith. They have forgotten the admonition that we are to "ask in faith, with no doubting, for he who doubts is like a wave of the sea, driven and tossed by the wind" (James 1:6).

Here is what I intend to teach my children about prayer.

Prayer has been a part of your life since you were an infant. Your mom and I have taken turns putting your chubby little hands together before you could even speak. As you grew you watched either your parents or older siblings lead prayer before meals. Your mom and I prayed for you before you were born, we prayed for you at night, and we will continue praying for you long after you leave our home. I hope that prayer becomes a natural part of your life.

Over and over in God's Word we have Biblical examples of Jesus—the Master Teacher—praying. For instance on one occasion we find Christ praying in the morning (Mark 1:35) or on the mountain (Matthew 14:23).

Prayer was such an important part of His life that He would frequently slip away so that He could spend time in prayer to His Father.

In Luke 11:1 we find the disciples asking Christ to teach them how to pray. Their request is then followed by Jesus reciting the model prayer—what many refer to as the Lord's Prayer. A close examination of Jesus' life finds Him praying for Himself on occasions (e.g., in the Garden of Gethsemane, Matthew 26; John 17:1-5) and praying for others (e.g., His disciples and for all believers, John 17). You would do well to follow His example.

Prayer will strengthen your relationship to God. How can you expect to have a good relationship with someone unless you talk to them? Let God know your joys and sorrows. When you were younger we discussed formatting your prayers around the acronym **ACTS**. **A**cknowledge the power and glory of God. **C**onfess sins and ask for forgiveness (Acts 8:22-24). **T**hank God for your countless blessings. And finally make your **S**upplications known to Him. As you got older we asked that you make prayer more personal and "put flesh on the skeleton." During His model prayer Jesus demonstrated praying for our daily needs (Matthew 6:11). Let me encourage you to use prayer as a weapon against temptation (Matthew 6:13; 26:41) and even pray for your enemies (Matthew 5:44). Pray for our leaders (both in the nation and in our church) and pray for those who are sick (spiritually and physically). Pray during good times and bad.

Make no doubt about it, prayer works! The Bible clearly indicates that if we are obedient God will answer our prayers (1 John 3:22-24; John 9:31). We must always remember to ask as Jesus did— "not my will, but Yours, be done" (Luke 22:42). Additionally, we must constantly remember that God knows the big picture, and so even though it may seem that He is not answering our prayers, or answering them the way we see fit, He is still in control and knows what is best. Let me encourage you to ask in faith, pray in faith, and relish your time in prayer with Him.

Love,

*"Do not be wise in your
own eyes; Fear the Lord
and depart from evil."
- Proverbs 3:7*

Fear This

Fear is not something adults like to reveal. Once the "monsters" have left our closets and we grow into adulthood, fear is often viewed as a sign of weakness. As such, the command to fear the Lord is often neglected. How often do you hear of someone expressing a healthy fear of God or working out their salvation with "fear and trembling" (Philippians 2:12)?

As baby-boomers expanded their hedonistic, rebellious spirit into our culture, the concept of reverence and fear of God was lost. They did not heed authority in any fashion—and for many that even included God. Subsequently the children of baby-boomers grew up never witnessing fear or reverence toward God. At the same time baby-boomers were rebelling, the embers from "hellfire and brimstone" sermons began dying down in pulpits all across the United States. The reverence and fear of God was replaced by "programs" and a newly recast God of only love and grace. Sermons emphasizing God's love and mercy took center stage as fear and reverence became outdated theology in many pulpits. But at what cost?

Here is what I intend to teach my children about fearing God.

I am so very thankful that we have a monster stick in our house— a special stick that is able to keep the monsters away at night. With that stick safely tucked beside your bed, I am able to stay in bed on nights when the fear of monsters creeps into your mind. While older individuals don't often admit it, you will learn that even adults have a fear of things like snakes, spiders, or enclosed spaces. While your mom and I both desire you to grow healthy and strong and leave childhood fears behind, we do hope you will retain one important fear—a fear of the Lord.

The Bible clearly records, "Let all the earth fear the Lord; Let all the inhabitants of the world stand in awe of Him" (Psalm 33:8). The inspired psalmist also recorded, "The Lord takes pleasure in those who fear Him, in those who hope in His mercy" (Psalm 147:11). The fear of the Lord will prolong your days (Proverbs 10:27). The Bible says over and over that the fear of the Lord is the beginning of wisdom. Consider the following inspired words: "The fear of the Lord is the beginning of wisdom: and the knowledge of the holy is understanding" (Proverbs 9:10). The inspired psalmist observed, "The fear of the Lord is the beginning of wisdom: a good understanding have all they that do His commandments: His praise endureth for ever" (Psalm 111:10; see also Proverbs 1:7). Thousands of individuals search for wisdom and knowledge in vain. They may learn trivia or memorize theories, but we must never forget that true wisdom comes from God.

I pray that you will serve the Lord with fear (Psalm 2:11) and maintain a healthy fear of Him during your lifetime. Never forget that the "fear of the Lord" is to hate evil (Proverbs 8:13). We read in Proverbs 14:26-27, "In the fear of the Lord there is strong confidence, and His children will have a place of refuge. The fear of the Lord is a fountain of life, to turn one away from the snares of death." Model yourself after the early New Testament Christians whom we know developed a healthy fear. "Then the churches throughout all Judea, Galilee, and Samaria had peace and were edified. And walking in the fear of the Lord and in the comfort of the Holy Spirit, they were multiplied" (Acts 9:31). Always preserve a healthy reverence for God (Isaiah 8:11-14).

It's important that you understand this is not a nightmare, terror-like fear in the absence of love. Remember God is love. Rather this is a serious fear that should motivate you and your actions. Without fear you will never be motivated to toward repentance. This is not a fear of God trying to trip you up or catch you doing wrong. As the inspired psalmist noted, "If You, Lord, should mark iniquities, O Lord, who could stand? But there is forgiveness with You, that You may be feared" (Psalm 130:3-4, emp. added). It is only with a healthy amount of fear that you can develop a proper relationship with God. Proverbs 19:23 notes, "The fear of the Lord leads to life, and he who has it will abide in satisfaction; He will not be visited with evil."

I encourage you to read Proverbs and Psalms to get a full understanding of the admonition to fear God. In your reading you will learn "God is greatly to be feared in the assembly of the saints, and to be held in reverence by all those around Him" (Psalm 89:7). Know that the remaining days you spend in our house we will continue to teach you this proper perspective. As the inspired psalmist observed, "Come, you children, listen to me; I will teach you the fear of the Lord" (Psalm 34:11).

Love,

"So that you incline your ear to wisdom, And apply your heart to understanding;"
- Proverbs 2:2

Elders

Titles within religious organization range from authorized to ostentatious. A quick glance at a local church sign might reveal "John Smith" as the pastor, preacher, cardinal, minister, saint, reverend, bishop, evangelist, or father. This bewilderment over titles often results in confusion of the actual role of particular church leaders. Even within the New Testament church there is oftentimes confusion over the terms pastor, elder, and preacher.

Another bit of confusion hinges on truth that many individuals forget there is a large difference between a "title" and a God-appointed position. A title alone bears no responsibility and is something someone wears to be seen—whereas a position is commonly something someone does. One is a label that men wear to be seen, while the other is often a servant lifestyle that affects one's actions. Many congregations bestow "titles" but the individual's life never reflects a change as they accept that new position.

The position of elder has, on occasion, split congregations because someone did (or did not) receive a particular title or position. Feelings get hurt and family lines get drawn as church members plead the case for "their guy." So what is an elder, and what does that position represent?

Here is what I intend to teach my children about elders.

In the secular world fancy-sounding titles are often easy to come-by, and hold very little actual value. Unless a particular "title" is used in the Bible then do not embrace it within the church. Look for Biblical examples of titles, and then take the next step and look for Scriptural examples of the jobs these men performed. An elder is a Biblical position in which one serves as an overseer for a local congregation. Most often elders are not preachers or evangelists, however this is not always the case.

Your mother and I are rearing you (boys) to one-day serve as elders in a local congregation. If we have done our job properly at home, then the concept of church elders should be easy to understand. Just as a father is to watch over, guard, spiritually feed, and protect his own children, this same thing takes place within a **church family**—with elders acting in the authoritative role. Just as I would correct and discipline you when you were young in order to save your soul, these men perform a similar duty. These are men who care for—and guard—the souls of the entire congregation. This is an enormous role, but one to which you should aspire to. The Bible indicates that these men "who rule well be counted worthy of double honor" (1 Timothy 5:17) and they will receive a "crown of glory that does not fade away" (1 Peter 5:4).

Historically, elders were ordained in churches once men were qualified. We have examples in the book of Acts as the New Testament church was growing of elders being ordained (see Acts 14:22-23; Acts 20:17; and Titus 1:5). These men—acting as a group—have authority over local congregations (1 Peter 5:2). The Bible indicates they are not to Lord this position over the congregation, but rather they are to set an example for the congregation (1 Peter 5:3), and lead the congregation in the direction Christ would have it go. Never forget that Jesus Christ is head of the church (Colossians 1:18; Ephesians 1:22-23). It is up to the elders of each congregation to uphold the truths that Jesus has revealed.

Elders go by many names in the New Testament. My favorite is "shepherd" (1 Peter 5:4). This designation implies that the men serving in this capacity are to feed and protect the flock. They are also referred to as bishops (1 Timothy 3:1-2), elders, (1 Timothy

5:17), presbyter (1 Timothy 5:1), pastor (Ephesians 4:11), and overseer (Acts 20:28). Spend a moment truly contemplating what each of these names really means. All of these names reflect the same office, and convey a description of their work. These men play a key role in God's plan for church government.

The Bible gives crystal clear qualifications that one should meet to be an elder (1 Timothy 3; Titus 1). One of the biggest mistakes local congregations can make is to install a "good man" who is not truly qualified. It is one thing to understand "business." It is entirely a different thing to have a working knowledge of God's Word and be able to defend it. While many churches use elders to "run" a local congregation and make business decisions, the Scriptures speak of a more important role. If you ever reach the position of an elder remember that there is a vast difference between gathering around a coffee table with members of your flock versus sitting around a conference table. I think many of the problems that arise in local congregations could be better resolved if qualified elders took a coffee table approach.

Listen, oh my children—when you leave home, find a congregation with strong sound elders. Find a congregation who has men who care about your souls and have the courage to stand up when something is wrong. Quiz them on their beliefs and I hope they will in turn question you regarding your past and beliefs. Find men who are knowledgeable of the Bible and make their decisions based on His precepts rather than on opinions, emotions, or financial concerns. With the right men holding the position of elders, the other things should properly fall into place, and problems will be Scripturally addressed.

Love,

Dad

"*He who gathers in summer is a wise son; He who sleeps in harvest is a son who causes shame.*"
- *Proverbs 10:5*

Deacons

There are so many things that Christians do that go unseen or unnoticed—oftentimes these are very essential works that are behind the scenes. Buildings are maintained, sick are visited, orphans and widows are cared for, programs are carried out, all because many Christians desire to be servants for Him. Oftentimes, these efforts never receive an official "thank you" from the pulpit. And yet, they still get done because of someone's love for God. Most people are very familiar with the 80/20 rule. This is the concept that 80 percent of the work is carried out by 20 percent of the people. I have had the pleasure of meeting and even working with individuals who are in the 20% that work hard. Ironically, I can't recall anyone who told me they belonged to the 80% who do little.

When it comes to rolling up sleeves and doing work some individuals would rather take a pass. It's hard for me personally to understand that disposition. As someone who regularly reflects on what Christ did for me, I have a burning passion to serve Him and be a better Christian with each new day. There are many weeks that I feel like I have not done enough! I would hope that all who wear the name "Christian" have a genuine desire to serve Him. One special group of individuals within the church actually wears the name "servants." The word deacon is derived from the Greek word *diakonos*, which is commonly translated "servant." These are men who have been selected to serve in particular capacities—usually taking advantage of specifics talents or fulfilling specific needs. Paul addressed his letter to the church at Philippi and included the deacons in his salutation (Philippians 1:1).

Here is what I intend to teach my children about deacons.

Heart of the Matter

In the September/October 2005 issue of The Futurist, the writers analyzed how we spend our time. Although almost every American would argue they don't have much free or leisure time, this study clearly demonstrated that we have roughly 35 hours per week of leisure time. That's approximately five hours per day that is frequently eaten up using the computer, watching television, reading, socializing, playing sports, or just relaxing. Consider for one moment what would happen if five of those leisure hours were given back to the church, and ten were dedicated to family. How much stronger would our families and church families be if we all devoted more time to them? Whether you ever wear the name "deacon," I expect you to use the time God gives you wisely and fulfill that role of being a busy servant.

God in His infinite wisdom designed an office in the church to help meet the needs of members in the local congregation. The specific qualifications for these men can be found in 1 Timothy 3:8-13. It is my prayer that my sons will long to serve as these special servants. These are men who are charged to take care of the physical welfare of the local congregation, which then allows the elders to focus on the spiritual welfare of the congregation. Consider what happens if elders are so busy worrying about building and grounds maintenance or audio/visual issues that they don't have time to consider the spiritual welfare of the congregation. In Acts 6 we see an instance where the widows were being neglected. The Twelve called the disciples together and asked them to select "men of good reputation" (vs. 3) who would allow the Apostles to continue studying and praying.

Understand that "deacon" is a description—servant—rather than a title. Far too often men get so caught up with titles and their "area/territory" that the work never gets done or things get bogged down. Occasionally men will argue over who is supposed to do something or make matters entirely too complex. For instance, in one congregation your mom and I attended, the elders asked the deacons to look into what it would take to create visitor parking places. This request came up several times over a period of a year in men's business meetings. (They actually formed a committee about it). One Sunday afternoon following yet another business meeting I called the elders and asked if I paid for it out of pocket could I just do it? Two hours and approximately $20 dollars later the task was done.

The office of deacon is a special office of service and one that I hope your heart will desire. Whether you wear the name "deacon" or not, stay busy serving Him.

Love,

"Happy is the man who finds wisdom, And the man who gains understanding;"
- Proverb 3:13

It's a Miracle ... or Is It?

The word itself has been cheapened by overuse and confusion today—that word is miracle. Headlines make bold declarations such as "Miracle on the Hudson River" or "Miracle Child Born" on a fairly regular basis. Being altruistic human beings who love a happy ending, we tend to gravitate toward these "good news" human interests stories. Hollywood has tried its best to cash in on this appeal by using the word miracle in some of the shows they produce. But are miracles really still happening today?

Rare is the individual who has not heard of a person who recovered from what was believed to be a deadly injury or terminal sickness. Occasionally, someone will even claim to be the recipient of a miraculous event or assert that he/she possesses miraculous gifts such as speaking in tongues or the power to heal or foretell the future. All of this attention has caused a tremendous amount of confusion and turmoil within Christianity.

Here is what I intend to teach my children on miracles.

You will meet individuals who laugh at the very notion of miracles. These are individuals who have been trained by the scientific method to believe that if you can't measure it with your five senses then it is not real. As a result of this scorn, many Christians try to steer clear of miracles for fear that they can't adequately defend them. Make no mistake about it, miracles did occur. If one were to remove all of the miraculous events from God's Word, then the entire message would ultimately be watered down and lost. A God that cannot perform miracles is no god at all. For many, Jesus walking on water or raising individuals from the dead represents the classic "textbook example" of a miracle, but understand that none of these miracles would have been possible had it not been for a significant miracle that occurred many years before. When Moses wrote in Genesis 1:1, "In the beginning God created the heavens and the earth," he summarized in a single sentence one of the most important miracles of all—the miracle of creation.

Before discussing whether miracles happen today, we need to make sure we completely understand the true definition of miracle.

A **real** miracle is something that is not only abnormal or unexplainable, but it is also **outside the natural forces of nature**.

The purpose of miracles has always been the same: to demonstrate the existence and power of God. With this in mind, we can look through God's Word and see countless examples of miracles such as Moses talking to the burning bush (Exodus 3:2), his parting the Red Sea (Exodus 14), Jonah being swallowed by a fish (Jonah 1:7-17), Balaam's mule speaking (Numbers 22:28); Jesus raising Lazarus from the dead, (John 11) Jesus walking on water (Matthew 14; Mark 6) and Jesus feeding the five thousand (Matthew 14).

After Jesus' resurrection, miraculous gifts were used by the Apostles to bring non-Christians to a full knowledge of the truth regarding God and Jesus Christ. For instance, on the day the very first Gospel sermon was preached (Pentecost), the Apostles were able to speak foreign languages of which they had no prior knowledge (Acts 2:4). They were also given the ability to heal people (Acts 3; Acts 14:8-11), raise the dead (Acts 9:36-42; 20:9ff), and could even confer miraculous gifts on to others (Acts 8:19; 19:1-6). Given that these men were working during a time when the Bible was not yet in a completed form as we have it today, those miraculous gifts were useful tools to help reveal and confirm what would one day become the written Word (see Hebrews 2:3-4).

But are miracles still happening today? Paul wrote that they would cease (1 Corinthians 13:8). In fact, Paul described their purpose and went on to give a timeline of expiration for them in Ephesians 4:11-13. With the death of the Apostles (and those individuals upon whom they had conferred special gifts), miracles ceased. Simply put, we don't need miracles to help confirm the truths of God today because we have the Bible. This doesn't mean that God has been handcuffed and cannot act in your life. But remember when people make claims of miraculous events today, stop and ask yourself, "Are these truly outside the laws of nature?" Was anyone raised from the dead or was sight restored to a blind person? Have arms or legs been regenerated for someone who was lame? Before casually tossing around that word *miracle*, remember what and Whom it represented in the past.

Love,

Dad

"The lips of the righteous know what is accept-able, But the mouth of the wicked what is perverse."
- Proverbs 10:32

"You Hypocrites ... "

"If that is what Christianity is all about, then I don't want to have anything to do with it!" Those words have punctuated **the end** for many individuals, as they permanently close the door on Christianity. They see or hear people behaving in a way that is in direct contradiction to how the Bible indicates Christians should act. As a result, these disillusioned individuals end up abandoning Christianity, not because of what the Bible says, but rather because of the actions of others. Only Heaven will reveal the number of souls that have been forfeited from faulting the hypocrisy of others. The anger and fury against hypocrisy has affected non-Christians, new Christians, and even mature Christians. In some cases, it has weakened people's faith; in others it has literally split congregations as individuals choose "sides."

Here is what I intend to teach my children about hypocrisy.

The word *hypocrite* is best defined as a false religious appearance. It is a word that you will hear during your lifetime, and it is a word I pray will **never be accurately charged to you**. Simply put, hypocrites are individuals who are Christians only in appearance, but not in deed. Remember it this way—the sin of hypocrisy is a heart problem dressed in nice clothes.

Your mother and I have taught you repeatedly (and will continue teaching you) the importance of possessing a heart for God. Our lips can utter the right words, we can carry out the right actions and wear the right clothes, but if our hearts are not truly convicted for God, then these actions are in vain. Jesus remarked on this when He quoted a passage from Isaiah (29:13) saying, "These people draw near to Me with their mouths, and honor Me with their lips, but their heart is far from Me" (Matthew 15:8). If you cultivate a heart for God, the right actions will follow!

But what about those individuals you witness saying one thing but doing something totally different? Always bear in mind that while God's plan (including the Church) is perfect, humans are not. We all make mistakes and sin (Romans 3:23). Never forget the Church is full of sinners! However, don't allow someone else's hypocrisy to interfere in **your** relationship with God. Remember, there will be no hypocrites or righteous individuals who are standing before God on your behalf. It will only be you (and Jesus Christ who will be there to confess you before Almighty God— Matthew 10:23).

Since hypocrites are not going to have anything to do with your defense on the Day of Judgment, do not dare allow them to weaken your relationship to God!

Jesus spoke harshly against the hypocrisy of the Pharisees (see Matthew 6:5; Matthew 22:18; Matthew 23). In Matthew 23 Jesus condemns the actions of the Pharisees, and during His message Jesus refers to these religious leaders as hypocrites several times. In verses 27-28 Jesus explains that the Pharisees are like "whitewashed tombs which indeed appear beautiful outwardly, but inside are full of dead men's bones and all uncleanness. Even so you also outwardly appear righteous to men, but inside you are full of hypocrisy and lawlessness." This is why we constantly remind Claire that we want her to be a pretty girl on the inside as well as outside! (That goes for you guys as well!)

Several years ago I spent some time evaluating my own life. I was aware of several individuals, preachers, and writers who were not **living outside** the pulpit what they were **preaching in** it. I didn't want to follow in their footsteps and have worked diligently to make sure what people see in the pulpit is the same Dad you see at home. The heart that individuals see on Sunday morning is the same heart I pour out before God at our home. My prayer is that each of you will be genuine Christians—Christians who occasionally make mistakes and who aren't perfect, but genuine Christians nonetheless. Fight hypocrisy with every fiber of your being! The Bible reminds us, "Therefore, laying aside all malice, deceit, hypocrisy, envy, and all evil speaking" (1 Peter 2:1, see also 1 Timothy 4:1-2). Paul wrote to the Christians in Rome admonishing, "Let love be without hypocrisy. Abhor what is evil. Cling to what is good" (Romans 12:9, see also James 3:17). Be the same on the inside and out!

Love,

Dad

Letters ...
Regarding Christian
Life and Home

Tolerate This!

At a recent seminar, a gentleman asked me what was so wrong with my children being educated about the Muslim religion in the public school system. His question mirrored the sentiments of many living today. Simply put, many people want us to be tolerant of everything. In fact, our children are being indoctrinated with the notion that the only real "sin" is the sin of intolerance. The mainstream media has done a phenomenal job of convincing our culture that we should accept all beliefs and all lifestyles, and to do otherwise is shameful. Anyone who dares not be totally accepting is considered narrow-mind- ed or judgmental. Today, many people have embraced the notion that one belief system is as good as another and that one religion is as good as another. You have your God, and I have mine. This idea of "total acceptance" and compromise has led many New Testament Christians to wonder if there really is one way, or will all "good people" go to Heaven?

Here is what I intend to teach my children about tolerance.

I pray that you grow up with a healthy dose of intolerance in your heart. Intolerance is not a sin. Consider that the very first commandment of the Ten Commandments was "Thou shall have no other gods before Me" (Exodus 20:3). Our God is a jealous God (Deuteronomy 4:24), and He will not tolerate you accepting or embracing other gods. As we look through the Bible, we see multiple exam- ples of individuals who were intolerant of unrighteousness. We know Elijah was intolerant of Jezebel (1 Kings 19). Paul was intolerant of witchcraft books (Acts 19:11-19). Peter was intolerant of the unrepentant Jews (Acts 2:37-39). Jesus, the Son of God, was intolerant of money-changers making the temple into a den of thieves (Mark 11:15-18). Jehovah God was intolerant of the vile homosexual behavior in Sodom and Gomorrah [Genesis 19—Don't forget, He even over-threw the inhabitants of the all the Cities of the Plain: Admah and Zeboim vs. 22 with the exception of Zoar, Deu. 29:23].

Many of the same people who are crying for mankind to tolerate everything have overlooked many examples of intolerance that have utterly reshaped the country in which we live. For instance, what would this country be like if George Washington had tolerated British troops? Where would we be today if Thomas Jefferson had tolerated King George III? What if Fredrick Douglas had tolerated slavery, or Martin Luther King Jr. had tolerated segregation? What would America be like if Winston Churchill had tolerated Adolf Hitler or if Susan B. Anthony tolerated only men voting? Part of what made these individuals great was that they were strong enough to stand up for their convictions. They recognized something as "wrong," and they didn't tolerate it.

This doesn't mean we are to be unkind or harsh—as there may be some occasions in which you find yourself having to tolerate a particular situation (e.g., drunk people at a ballgame who paid money for a seat just like you.) We are always to live our lives as Christians, but we can still recognize things that are good and right versus those that are not. Tolerance of all beliefs means you don't perceive any- thing as a standard for "right" or "wrong." This embracing of everything ultimately means we are giving our ap- proval to whatever behavior, belief, or lifestyle people choose.

Never forget, Jesus Christ said, "I am the way, the truth, and the life. No one comes to the Father except through Me" (John 14:6). That's not a question of tolerance ... it's a statement of Truth! Those who profess a belief in God or Christianity need to grasp the inflexibility of that statement. There is only one Way—pe- riod! You will meet many "good people" in your lifetime who may earnestly desire to go to Heaven instead of Hell, but unless they "tolerate" and submit to the Words of the Son of God and obey Him, they will be lost. For those who believe this is judgmental, we should ask them why they question the Creator's plan—are they intolerant to Him and His scheme of redemption for eternal salvation?

Love,

"Children's children are the crown of old men, And the glory of children is their father."
- Proverbs 17:6

Children are a Blessing

The difference is palpable—and tragic. Watch a visiting family with two young children enter a church building and the response you witness is overwhelming. People go out of their way (literally) to meet these new visitors and share with them what their congregation has to offer children. But consider for a moment the response to a family who walks in, followed behind by six or seven children. The response is not as overwhelming. In fact, she is often viewed as odd, irresponsible, not financially wise, lower class, or socially ignorant. More often than not, Christians steer very clear of extremely large families. After all, society has successfully convinced us that "two" is the magic number for children. (Of course, there is the unwritten rule that you can try one more time if the first two were the same sex.) Even from the pulpit we hear a preacher joking about "the close call" of him and his wife thinking they might be pregnant. Fact of the matter is this is not a joking subject.

How sad is it to hear a preacher teach a powerful lesson on children and the home only to realize that his actions are teaching a totally different lesson. I have listened firsthand to a preacher give counsel about the "wisdom" of only having one or two children—and that anything more than that is "foolish." This same preacher would then mount the pulpit and preach a tear-jerking lesson on Psalm 127 and children. While his voice spoke one message, his life and his actions spoke an entirely different message. There are some Christians who need to really re-evaluate their view of children in the light of God's Word.

Here is what I intend to teach my children about the blessings

of children.

Not a morning passes by in our house when your mom and I are not thankful for the sounds of little feet and tender young voices. We feel incredibly blessed by God to have children, and we pray that you will be able to experience the same joys of parenthood.

I'm not exactly sure of the precise date of when children went from being considered a blessing to being considered baggage, but, unfortunately, I have witnessed it countless times. Parents, oftentimes, view the existence of their children as competition for their own personal desires and wishes. **At some point along the way, parents began to value prosperity more than posterity.** I hope that you will **boldly reject society's view** of children. Never look upon children as a burden or an expense. Sure, we need to be financially responsible—but children are not a tally mark we put under the "expense" column.

Sadly, many parents today do not even like their children. The responsibility for rearing these children is given to anyone and everyone—except their own parents (see Deuteronomy 6:4-9—a passage directed toward parents). In some homes, children are treated as just another piece of property, a commodity, or a show-piece to be trotted out when guests visit. Parents have forgotten that they are responsible to return the souls of their children to God, and that every soul is precious (Matthew 16:24-26).

Every time you see a child's face, I hope that the first thought that enters your mind will be "a blessing from God." The inspired psalmist observed, "Behold, children are a heritage from the Lord, the fruit of the womb is a reward" (Psalm 127:3). It then continues by saying, "Happy is the man who has his quiver full of them." When you see a family enter a church building with many children, I hope you will remind yourself and that mother how blessed she truly is. Solomon wrote, "Children's children are the crown of old men, and the glory of children is their father" (Proverbs 17:6). I'm looking forward to that crown! While I don't know God's plan for each one of you, I do pray you enjoy parenthood—whether it be you physically having children or adopting little ones into your family. I wish for you a full quiver so that you too can experience the love, joys, and happiness that you have brought your mother and me.

Love,

Dad

"Train up a child in the way he should go, and when he is old he will not depart from it."
- Proverbs 22:6

Giver vs. Taker

It's no secret that we live in a materialistic society. The mainstream media constantly bombards us with advertisements of products that we "need." My generation has perfected the art of "keeping up with the Joneses." In fact, most individuals my age wanted to start their marriages with the same material possessions our parents took thirty years to amass. And so we purchased it all—on credit. We are a generation of consumers and takers. Sadly, this selfishness is now being passed on to future generations, as children want more and more. Holidays such as Christmas are no longer about family and memories, but rather they revolve around commercialism and "things."

Here is what I intend to teach my children about giving versus taking.

Every Christmas morning since you were born, your mother and I have set up a video camera to record the events of the morning. It's one of the ways we have recorded you growing up through the years, as you went from crawling over presents and playing with empty boxes, to running into the room trying to guess exactly what was in each box. One of our joys as parents has been watching you tear open the wrapping paper and seeing your eyes light up as you see what is contained in the package.

Having been reared in the United States you are extremely blessed. You have never experienced poverty or not had something you need. In fact, most of the time you get things you want. But your mother and I worry about what we are teaching you regarding giving versus taking. One of my greatest hopes is that during your lifetime you will learn the joy of giving. Undoubtedly, you will grow up around individuals who surround themselves with "things."

But remember things won't buy happiness. Remember that those "things" can never fill the void in your life like He can. And never forget, ultimately, Who owns everything.

There are literally thousands of individuals who have abandoned the faith in favor of material possessions. These people are selfish takers. They never learned the art of giving. In the book of Acts, Paul reminded the people of the words Jesus Christ had shared, saying, "It is more blessed to give than to receive" (Acts 20:35). Never forget this admonition from the Son of God. I pray that as you grow older you will constantly be on the lookout for ways to **give** to others. The feeling you get inside is like none other. Practice random acts of kindness. Never forget — people are much more valuable than things.

When your mom and I were in Russia, we had the opportunity to visit the "flat" (apartment) of one of the local Christians. They lived a beautiful life, but it was obvious they did not own near the material possessions we did. They worked hard just to get by. During our visit, we complimented a picture she had hanging on the wall, and she literally went over and took it off the wall and gave it to us. We tried desperately to tell her no, but she insisted. In the years since I have forgotten her name but we still have the picture. Her act of kindness has remained in my memory for years. She truly was a giver.

As you mature you will meet people who place an inordinate amount of attention on material possessions. Their identity is shaped not by who they really are, but rather by what they own. Many people spend years climbing the corporate ladder so that they can buy more "things." These individuals remind us of the rich young ruler who asked Jesus what he needed to do to have eternal life. "Jesus said to him, 'If you want to be perfect, go sell what you have and give to the poor, and you will have treasure in Heaven; and come and follow Me'" (Matthew 19:21). Rather than him ruling his possessions, his possessions ruled him. The Bible tells us he went away sorrowful because he had many possessions. Be thankful for God's blessing to you, but never let your material possessions separate you from Jehovah God. Look for ways to share your possessions. Be a giver, not a taker!

Love,

*"Go to the ant, you slug-
gard! Consider her ways
and be wise,"
- Proverbs 6:6*

Work is not a Dirty Word

Christians have a reputation. No, not *that* reputation regarding Christ. This is a different reputation—one that is less than pleasant. This is a reputation of which many are quite aware and on which some have even commented on. It's the reputation of being cheap and not working as hard. Before you get too upset, allow me to explain.

On more than one occasion I have heard business people (Christians and non-Christians) remark that they had rather work for anyone other than a Christian. How tragic is that?! This is usually followed with a description of how Christians always want a discounted bill, expect better than average work, and yet they, oftentimes, are the slowest to pay their bills. I suspect many Christians believe they are entitled to a reduced price—especially if the work is being done by another Christian—and they assume that they can simply "pay when they want."

On the flip side of this coin, there are Christian employees who approach jobs half-heartedly, not really giving their boss a full day's work for a full day's wage. They are happy with doing the "minimum" (or less). These may be individuals who believe they are underpaid or who regularly attend to personal issues during work hours. They often work simply so they can play. In addition, you have some Christians who perform work for the Church (e.g., helping maintain the building, computers, lawn, pest control, preschool, etc.) who see no problem in cutting corners—because after all, it's the Church.

Here is what I intend to teach my children about work ethic.

Heart of the Matter

I started working when I was twelve years old. My first jobs were mowing grass and cooking/catering meals through high school (Yes, I can cook and also decorate wedding cakes!). I have been working in some form or fashion ever since those initial jobs. Work is a healthy part of life for which you need to be prepared. It is a good thing to be able to earn a wage, care for a home, and provide for your family. It has been a part of God's plan from the very beginning. While many believe Adam didn't have to do anything in the Garden of Eden, the Bible indicates that he was to tend and keep the garden that God had created (Genesis 2:15). After the fall of man in Genesis 3, we find that Adam would now sweat at his job until he died (3:19).

Your mom and I are working hard to create a good work ethic in each one of you. That goes for both males and females. Just because a woman works within the home does not mean she is not "working." (In fact, I have said many times that your mother works harder than I do as she tends our home.) Our task is to prepare you Claire to be a hard-working homemaker like your mother and to prepare you boys to earn a wage to provide for your families. I often refer to our house as a ship, and part of your mother's job is to make sure that ship stays afloat and heading in the right direction. She is incredible at what she is able to do. Her tasks are not easy, and they will be important for Claire to learn as she prepares to become a homemaker herself. You would all do well to learn from your mother and pattern your own homes after hers.

A good work ethic is hard to find these days, and it is one reason you were introduced to chores at a fairly young age in life. Sometimes, it is not so much the chore with which we are concerned, but rather that you are learning a work ethic and a proper attitude. In Ecclesiastes 9:10 we read, "Whatever your hand finds to do, do it with your might." We expect you to be an honest, diligent, and hard-working employee. We want you to be the type of individual that employers crave—and we know that you can be. God has instilled in each one of you talents and abilities that you can use for Him, but also in a work environment. Consider the strong warning Paul gave the Christians at Thessalonica:

"nor did we eat anyone's bread free of charge, but worked with labor and toil night and day, that we might not be a burden to any of you, not because we do not have authority, but to make ourselves an example of how you should follow us. For even when we were with you, we commanded you this: If anyone will not work, neither shall he eat. For we hear that there are some who walk among you in a disorderly manner, not working at all, but are busybodies." (2 Thessalonians 3:8-11)

Never forget that idleness will bring about problems.

Another lesson you need to learn sooner rather than later is that work is not all about money. Yes, it is nice to be paid a good wage for hard work (1 Timothy 5:18), but that is not all there is to life. There are untold thousands of individuals who have high-paying careers, but who also have high blood pressures, strained marriages, and Godless lives to prove it. I could have chosen other career paths that would have paid more—but I can assure each one of you that I would not have been as happy. And I would not have been at home as much as I am now. Your mom will attest that most mornings I am literally either singing in the shower or whistling as I head out the door because I am so happy to do what I do. (True, the singing is not a pretty sound, but you get the picture!) There is much to be said for the man who drives to work with a smile on his face and who can sleep soundly every night.

One of my greatest hopes is that you will find a job that you enjoy and one that employs your talents in a way that is beneficial to His kingdom. You have heard us say many times that you can do just about anything you put your mind to, and we firmly believe that. As long as you are working hard and using your talents, we will be proud of whatever career path you choose. Find something at which you excel and do it with all your might for Him.

Make sure whatever you end up doing that you take God with you. There are too many individuals who forget their Christian examples when they are in the workplace. You have heard me preach about Christianity being the life you live and not just a label you wear. If it is truly the life you are living, then you will carry it with you into your workplace. Remember, you were created unto good works (Ephesians 2:10) and are to be zealous in those good works (Titus 2:14). We are called to abound in the work of the Lord (1 Corinthians 15:58) and be an example of good works (Titus 2:7). As you conduct yourself in the business world, do not forget that your actions (your work, repayment, attitude, etc.) are to reflect

Jesus Christ.

And finally, if you use a Christian to get a job done, pay him for his time—and pay him on time. Don't get into the habit of expecting things for free. If you own a business, do your best not to have bills past due. Be an example in everything that you do so that you can influence others for Him. And by the way, pick up your clothes...

Love,

Dad

"That you may preserve discretion, And your lips may keep knowledge." - Proverbs 5:2

Modesty

It's an epidemic that affects almost every congregation in the United States—immodesty. Clothing that was once reserved for immoral individuals is now considered "in style." Simply put—skin is in. Any clothing that isn't revealing skin is often so tight-fitting that one can easily spot moles or scars beneath the clothes. Sadly, many Christians have embraced this pagan practice and can see nothing wrong with imitating the world. In all of my years of teaching, this topic elicits more emotion from youth and their parents, as individuals seek to justify their clothing because they "can't find anything in the stores" or "my child has a wcird body type." And so week after week our children march into worship looking no different from the world, looking as though they were streetwalkers from the 1970s. It would be easy to get upset at these young people—however, it is the parents who most often purchase the clothes. And a quick scan around the auditorium reveals that some parents are trying their best to mimic the latest styles as well.

Imagine the scenario of watching a man serving the Lord's Supper, only to see him return to the front and place the bread plate on the table after only serving half of the auditorium. How would it feel to know the man stopped serving the Lord's Supper because he could not, in good conscience, continue looking up and down the aisle at people who were sitting in immodest clothing revealing far too much as he stood at the end of the row. There is no excuse for what is happening in our worship assemblies, and there is no excuse for elders and preachers not rebuking parents (and teens) for immodesty.

Here is what I intend to teach my children about immodesty.

Styles come and go. You may never experience wide collars or bell-bottom pants, but rest assured certain things will be "in style" in your life that the media wants you to embrace. There will be strong pressure to conform to the latest fads. But remember, it's just a fad. Sadly, many of your friends will find their self-worth in their clothes (brand name or style). I pray that we rear you to be more confident than that. Your self-worth is in the knowledge that you were bought with the blood of Jesus Christ!

Clothing began in the Garden of Eden. After eating of the tree of knowledge of good and evil, Adam and Eve covered themselves with fig leaves (Genesis 3:7). It is noteworthy to notice that after God pronounced His punishment on their sin, He further clothed them with tunics of skin (Genesis 3:21). From that point on, man has covered himself in the sight of others and in the sight of God. Clothing has been a part of life since those days in the Garden.

Jesus reminded us not to worry about clothes (Matthew 6:28-30), and as such, your mom and I don't put a huge emphasis on clothing. Yes, we want them to be clean. And yes, we'd prefer they fit— even though that is getting harder as growth spurts outpace your clothing sizes. But in your closet you will find some "outdated" outfits that still have lots of wear in them—and even some hand-me-downs that a sibling or friend once wore. That doesn't change who you are.

Modern styles change every season. The primary reason for these frequent changes is to drive sales up in the clothing market. Christians should recognize a problem with this constantly changing industry.

God does not change (Malachi 3:6), and neither does His view on modesty. Tight, low-cut, or revealing clothing is never "in style" in the sight of God.

Furthermore, just because you see another Christian wearing something does not necessarily mean it is appropriate. Christians are admonished to adorn themselves modestly (1 Timothy 2:9-10) and that beauty should not come from outward adornment (1 Peter 3:3-4). When selecting clothes I hope that you will select something that is glorifying to God and that does not draw undue attention. Our clothing should not cause anyone to lust (see Matthew 5:27-28).

You mom and I will not always be around to select or purchase (thankfully!) your clothes. It is my prayer that when you select something, you will remember Whose you are and Who you represent. Sure, you can dress like the world and blend in, but you are called to be different (Romans 12:1-2). That doesn't mean weird—but different. In a world determined to reveal skin, it shouldn't be hard to adopt a modest style that help demonstrate your Christian character. I assure you that wise clothing choices will earn you respect in the eyes of faithful men and women. Don't worry about the look and label on the outside. **Worry about your look and label on the inside!**

Love,

Dad

"Put away from you a deceitful mouth, And put perverse lips far from you."
- Proverbs 4:24

Just a Little White Lie

Lying and deceit have become commonplace in our society. Far too commonplace! Young and old alike have calloused themselves into believing that as long as no one is "hurt," then little white lies (or even occasionally bigger dark ones) are okay. It happens so often that many individuals never think twice about lying to coworkers, family, or friends. Add to this that politicians, advertisers, and the marketing world in general are constantly bombarding us with products and sales gimmicks that never live up to the promises. Entire businesses now have strategy meetings on how to deceive clients into thinking they are getting a better deal. Sadly, this lying and deceitful behavior is not limited to non-Christians.

Here is what I intend to teach my children about lying and deceit.

I pray that I'm with you on the day that it happens because I know it is coming. The day will come that someone you trusted will lie to you. I speak from experience, as I have had individuals very close to me lie, only to later find out they had deceived me repeatedly—for years. It hurts, and it's something that is not easy to forget.

Trust is not something that is easily earned or something that can be purchased. Trust is one of the most vital elements in a relationship—especially your marriage. When someone lies to me it affects our relationship for a long time, as that trust was shattered. I know you want to be trusted by us, and we want to trust you—so keep that in mind before telling an "innocent little white lie." Think long and hard before you ever violate the trust someone has put into you. Always let your word be your bond.

Heart of the Matter

Even in day-to-day activities of life. Don't make promises you can't keep—someone is counting on you to stand by your word. Don't lie online in a "profile" page or when answering the phone. Never fall into the pattern of taking your words lightly. Do everything you can to earn the trust of Christians and non-Christians alike. Because once those wicked habits slip in they are hard to eradicate. When you contemplate how to respond to people consider the following passages Matthew 15:18-20; Ephesians 4:15-16; Luke 8:15; Romans 12:17-21.

Your mother and I have always taught you that you will get in far more trouble for lying to us than if you just admitted to the situation. It may seem like lying will easily extinguish a problem, but I guarantee it will only make matters worse. Oftentimes, individuals who tell a lie to cover something, find themselves forced to lay down an entire web of lies to maintain their story. While you may temporarily escape a punishment for having done something wrong, you'll then have to live with the knowledge that you can no longer be trusted. Never forget, God doesn't lie (Numbers 23:19) and neither should we!

While the lie itself is a bad thing, your mom and I are worried about the deeper issue—that is your heart. Your mother and I have tried hard to fashion each of you with tender hearts—hearts that will be pricked by your conscience if you do something wrong. Most people lie because of one of three things: fear, greed, or pride. These conditions indicate serious heart problems. I pray that we have laid the groundwork that will cause your conscience to ache should you ever consider telling anyone a lie.

The Bible has nothing good to say about those who lie. In Proverbs 6, the writer outlines seven things God hates. One of those is a lying tongue (Proverbs 6:16-19). When Moses handed down the Ten Commandments, the ninth commandment declared, "You shall not bear false witness against your neighbor" (Exodus 20:16). Paul, in writing to the Christians in Colosse admonished "Do not lie to one another, since you have put off the old man" (Colossians 3:9-10). In fact, the Bible describes the devil as the father of lies (John 8:44). In Revelation 21:8 we read, "Liars shall have their part in the lake which burns with fire and brimstone." Lying will ultimately cost you your soul—a high price to pay for a "little white lie." Don't do it.

And for those rare occasions when your mom or wife asks, "Does this dress make me look fat?"— always remember to compliment her shoes!

Love,

Dad

"Wine is a mocker, Strong drink is a brawler, And whoever is led astray by it is not wise."
- Proverbs 20:1

Alcoholism

Some of the most creative advertising minds in the world are using their talents for the alcoholic beverage industry. Their commercials entertain millions while quietly planting seeds of desire. Magazine ads frequently portray the illusion of youthful pleasure and inclusion for those who drink alcohol. Research studies are frequently used as a tool to promote the benefits of drinking alcohol. But this beautiful mirage is clouded by a war that rages between the perceived "fun" of social drinking versus the ever-present danger of drunk driving and the reality of alcoholism. This is a war with extremely high stakes. On the one hand, lives are literally at risk, and on the other, beverage alcohol is a multi-billion dollar industry.

The controversy surrounding alcoholic beverages has found its way into the church as well. Scholarly men debate various Scriptures to either denounce or support drinking alcohol. Many congregations have quietly—almost unknowingly—segregated into clicks consisting of those who drink "socially" and those who don't. Members argue the ethics of investing in beer companies that are making huge profits. Both sides go to great strides to justify their positions. This tension has caused many preachers and elders to remain silent and comfortably "settle in" or ignore the issue altogether.

Here's what I intend on teaching my children about beverage alcohol.

I have been the "gatekeeper" monitoring what is introduced into your lives since you were born. In addition, your mother and I have been striving diligently to make sure that you were fed spiritually while under our roof. But I recognize that one day you will walk through that "gate" and I will turn these tasks over to you.

When that day arrives, you will determine what things you allow through the gate. I hope that alcoholic beverages are not one of those.

When you reach the age of twenty-one, our government has declared it legal for you to drink beer, wine, and liquor. (Don't lose sight of the fact that it is against the law before that time.) A common "right of passage" for individuals who reach this milestone is to go out and drink with friends. Let me strongly encourage you to find a better way to celebrate.

As you mature into adulthood, you will hear Christians argue about alcohol in the Bible. Many will correctly say the word *oinos* (wine) can mean alcoholic wine (Proverbs 20:1; Proverbs 23:31-35). Others correctly point out that the same word can mean juice from grapes (Isaiah 65:8; Isaiah 16:10). I've listened to some extremely wise men argue both sides that Jesus' first recorded miracle of making water into wine at the wedding in Cana (John 2:1-10) was either alcoholic or simply grape juice. People in favor of drinking alcohol will point out Scripture like 1 Timothy 3:8 that says one should not be given to "much wine"—stressing the "much" or that a little is good for the stomach (1 Timothy 5:23). These individuals will also point out that the Bible doesn't condemn drinking alcohol, but rather drunkenness.

A couple of things that I want to point out to help you fully understand this debate. First, individuals of that day were connoisseurs of grapes. Many men could probably tell you from what region the grapes were grown simply from the taste. Secondly, clean water was not as prevalent as we have it here in the United States. Men living during this time in history didn't have running water in their homes that had been chlorinated. In many regions—just like today—poor water would lead to sickness. As such, it was common for men to drink fruit juice with their meals. But refrigerators were also unknown at this time—so they needed a way to preserve juice and be able to drink it days or weeks after the juice was squeezed from the grapes.

The process of fermentation allowed the juice to be stored for much longer periods of time. (I would point out to you that the alcohol content in their "wine" was **much** less than what is used in wine today.)

As I mentioned, I know the controversy exists—and the debate will likely rage on long after I'm gone. It is your mother's and my prayer that you will throw all of the debate completely out the window and consider one thing: influence. As a faithful Christian, you must always consider how your influence affects others. What message are you sending the person from whom you purchase alcohol, or the individual who watches you carry it out of the store? This is one of those controversies that never needs to be a controversy. Rather than fret about alcoholism or justification of moderate drinking, just determine today that you will not use alcoholic beverages. It will make your life simpler and your influence stronger. Make a difference and be that shining light. You don't need it to be pleasing to God. As Paul admonished, "Abstain from every form of evil" (1 Thessalonians 5:22). I challenge you to be a gatekeeper who doesn't allow alcoholic beverages through your gate!

Love,

"For the Lord gives wisdom; From his mouth come knowledge and understanding;"
- Proverbs 2:6

Textbooks

By the time a child graduates from high school he or she will have digested the material contained in at least forty-five "textbooks." This number does not include extra reading or collegiate textbooks. Students find themselves weighed down with heavy backpacks filled with books published by companies like McGraw Hill, Prentice Hall, and Harcourt Brace. The goal is to memorize what is in the textbook and pass the test. The No Child Left Behind Act of 2001 has changed many classrooms into standardized testing preparation rooms with the textbooks being the study template. Students read through chapters of their textbooks and memorize trivia that will be regurgitated at some later testing date.

Children raised in Christian homes don't just learn their *ABCs* and *123s* from those textbooks. Tucked in with the reading, writing, and arithmetic are many statements promoting humanism, atheism, and evolution. Unfortunately, we in the church either have not caught on to this or are afraid to question the material. Maybe it's because things were not as bad when we were in school, because we know some Christian educators, or becuase we are told teachers skip certain bad chapters. But that doesn't change the very real fact that our children are getting a strong (and yearly) dose of secular material from textbooks that is not in accordance with God's Word. Add to this that we have a priority problem— how many times have parents skipped Bible study on Wednesday night because of all the secular homework a child brought home (or sports activities)? (Have you ever heard of a student staying home from school because they did not have their Bible class work finished?) Do we ever really consider the eternal cost? As Charles Francis Potter, co-signer of the *Humanist Manifesto*, noted: "Education is thus a most powerful ally of humanism, and every American public school is a school of humanism. What can the theistic Sunday schools, meeting for an hour once a week and teaching only a fraction of the children, do to stem the tide of a five-day program of humanistic teaching?" (1930, p. 128).

Here is what I intend to teach my children about textbooks.

I love to learn. As you know from watching me day to day, I have a book in my hand quite often around the house. Our home and my office are filled with textbooks on a broad variety of topics. But there is one major component you must never forget when considering the material found within your textbooks. **Textbooks—even good textbooks—contain errors and were written by fallible men!**

You will meet many people who put a great deal of emphasis on book learning and have either consciously or subconsciously placed their faith in textbooks. I pray that by now you have come to the realization that **God knows everything**. God knows everything about biology, geometry, astronomy, and even English! The inspired psalmist wrote, "He counts the number of stars; He calls them all by name. Great is our Lord, and mighty in power. His understanding is infinite" (Psalm 147:4-5). Truth be told, humans don't know a fraction of a fraction of a fraction of what God knows. That being the case, shouldn't we put our allegiance in the one book in which He communicates His knowledge to us—the Bible? While textbooks are nice, they can't compare to the accuracy and the truths found within the pages of God's Word. Never forget this. You can always count on the Bible to hold the Truth!

So, what is one to do when you read material in textbooks that contradicts what the Bible says? Always remember who ultimately knows more—God! Paul exhorted Timothy, "O Timothy! Guard what was committed to your trust, avoiding the profane and idle babblings and contradictions of what is falsely called knowledge [KJV-science]" (1 Timothy 6:20). Books are good to help you build knowledge using the brain God gave you—but remember as you grow in wisdom and stature Who knows everything.

Also enter your education knowing that there are "wolf statements" (see Matthew 10:16; Acts 20:29) written by men who do not believe in a God and are doing their very best to convert you to their godless belief system. In his book *Darwin's Dangerous Idea*, Daniel Dennett addressed parents who would teach their children something other than organic evolution: "Those of us who have freedom of speech will feel free to describe your teachings as the spreading of falsehoods, and will attempt to demonstrate this to your children at our earliest opportunity." The way in which they intend to do this is through textbooks that teach their belief system. Remember what Paul wrote in 1 Corinthians 3:19, "For the wisdom of this world is foolishness with God." When Adolf Hitler was laying the foundation for his New World Order—the Nazi Party—he commented, "Let me control the textbooks and I will control the state. The state will take youth and give to youth its own education and its own upbringing." John J. Dunphy knew this when he wrote his infamous article "A Religion for a New Age," in which he boldly proclaimed:

"I am convinced that the battle for humankind's future must be waged and won in the public school classroom by teachers who correctly perceive their role as the proselytizers of a new faith: a religion of humanity that recognizes the spark of what theologians call divinity in every human being. There teachers must embody the same selfless dedication of the most rabid fundamentalist preacher, for they will be ministers of another sort, utilizing a classroom instead of a pulpit to convey humanist values in whatever subject they teach, regardless of the educational level—preschool, daycare, or large state university. The classroom must and will become an arena of conflict between the old and the new—the rotting corpse of Christianity, together with all its adjacent evils and misery, and the new faith of humanism, resplendent in its promise of a world in which the never-realized Christian ideal of "love thy neighbor" will finally be achieved" (1983, p. 26).

Some parents will think I missed the mark on this one. They may call me an alarmist, or unrealistic about life. Go back and read about spiritual wisdom versus worldly wisdom (1 Corinthians 2-3). Some will point out textbooks are required to advance through school—and I would agree that you need a certain amount of book knowledge. However, having witnessed firsthand the results of ungodly indoctrination—and more lost souls than I can now keep up with—I wanted to remind you of what must be your number one priority and how to view man-written textbooks. Remember what Dad tells you—while you may be required to give the correct answers on a test, you don't have to drink the kool-aid!

Love,

Dad

"My son, do not despise the chastening of the Lord, Nor detest His correction; For whom the Lord loves He corrects, Just as a father the son in whom he delights."
- Proverbs 3:11-12

Discipline

Methods of child discipline "evolve" as our culture continues to change and drift. Popular books and trends have a way of setting a standard that can last for two or three generations. For instance, many of today's grandparents can remember Dr. Spock's Baby and Childcare and his advice on how to rear children. The concept of "time out" really took root during my generation—a concept that was completely foreign to our grandparents. Ironically, this is a topic that affects everyone but that is rarely discussed.

It is no secret that discipline has become much more lax in the past few decades. Corporal punishment has almost gone the way of the dinosaur in most school systems. I doubt the average parent has any idea the amount of red tape and paperwork involved in administering a spanking in public schools today. Under the guise of "love" and anti-abuse, many areas of the world have already outlawed spanking. This anti-spanking trend appears to be gaining ground and picking up speed.

Public pressure has all but silenced Christians. Many Christians now find themselves worried that any public display of discipline may resort in Child Protective Services removing their children from the home. To compound the problem, pulpits have stopped preaching specifics in this area and are now content to suggest vague generalities. We will readily condemn homosexuals and atheists, but we have forgotten that Paul put those who are disobedient to parents into the same chapter as the homosexuals and haters of God (Romans 1:28-30).

Here is what I intend to teach my children about discipline.

I will likely never forget the occasion in which I had to get you all out of bed and "line you all up" and administer a spanking. (And I suspect you might not forget it as well.) Earlier in the day I had mentioned that there would be a punishment if you all did not do something your mom and I requested. During my nightly check of the house, I realized that what we requested had gone undone. You will likely never know how badly I wanted to just do it myself and go on. It would have been so quick and easy. But I knew I couldn't. I loved you too much. And so through sobs and tears, I spanked each one of you—as a reminder to be obedient.

You know we believe in spanking. Each one of you has felt the swats and seen the dreaded "wooden spoon." The concept of "time out" is kind of a joke in our household. I have told you on more than one occasion that if my parents had put me in time out I would have simply used that time to figure out how not to get caught the next time! We have tried to convey discipline in a Biblical fashion, and have worked hard not to ever punish you in anger. While this may be hard to understand, we spank you because we love you dearly and want you to go to Heaven! That is why I try to remember to tell you I love you and why I am disciplining you when the need arises.

Spanking is a forgotten tool in modern times. Many people are afraid that it might be abusive or scar children emotionally. However, your mom and I believe the Bible is a lot smarter than any "self-help" book or current trend. Solomon in his wisdom declared, "He who spares his rod hares his son, but he who loves him disciplines him promptly" (Proverbs 13:24). Later on he cautioned, "Do not withhold correction from a child, for if you beat him with a rod, he will not die. You shall beat him with a rod and deliver his soul from hell" (Proverbs 23:13-14). I have listened to many Bible "scholars" try to put a different spin on these verses, suggesting that it is not actually talking about spanking children.

These are the same people who fight hard to defend other Truths found in God's Word. Those verses are not hard to understand, and they don't change over time. (Consider also Proverbs 22:15). Solomon warned, "Chasten your son while there is hope, and do not set your heart on his destruction (Proverbs 19:18). Now contrast that with a statement he wrote earlier: "My son, do not despise the chastening of the Lord, nor detest his correction; for whom the Lord loves He corrects, just as a father the son in whom he delights" (Proverbs 3:11). My prayer is that one day the relationship and discipline you have learned from me will be transferred into your relationship with your Heavenly Father.

On a few occasions you have heard your parents say, "Their parents must not love them as much as we love you" when discussing what someone else "gets away with" or poor behavior. While this may not make logical sense now, in time I guarantee it will. During your life you will see countless examples of young people who have ruined their lives in folly. They are literally bringing shame to their parents. The Proverb writer noted: "The rod and rebuke give wisdom, but a child left to himself brings shame to his mother" (29:15).

Thankfully, we have entered a stage in life where spanking has tapered off. God's way worked! The Bible told us, "Correct your son, and he will give you rest; yes, he will give delight to your soul (Proverbs 29:17). I am thankful that your obedience is now giving us delight. I pray you will reflect back and choose God's way for your children one day.

Love,

Letters ...
Regarding Your
Personal Growth

That's Not Fair

Anyone who has reared children, taught school, or run an office has heard the phrase: "That's not fair." In almost every instance in which a child makes a request to his or her parents, the child has already determined the response he wants to hear. Anything short of their desired response is considered unfair. Oftentimes their friends are unexpectedly brought into the picture as we hear: "But Steve/Beth gets to go." In fact, most parents (and even some bosses) can relate to being compared to others in a negative light. Children (and employees) are not afraid to tell us how much "nicer, kinder, sweeter, friendlier" other children's parents (or bosses) are. Rare is the home that has reared a teenager without having a bedroom door slammed followed by the words "That's not fair!" reverberating throughout the house.

Here is what I intend to teach my children about fairness.

Life is not always fair. I realize that this simple statement may catch you off guard or may not sit well with you, but it is the truth. There will be times in your life that you should win something, but due to forces outside of your control, it will go to someone else. There will be times that others around you are enjoying certain things that you will not have. There will be times you place your trust in someone who deceives you. But I want to make sure you understand something—that does not change who you are and Whom you serve.

Make no mistake: God is still in control, and He knows everything. Even on your most unfair day, you can take comfort in knowing He is still on His throne watching everything that transpires. The writer of Hebrews noted, "And there is no creature hidden from His sight, but all things are naked and open to the eyes of Him to whom we must give an account" (4:13; c.f. Proverbs 15:11; Romans 8:27). God knows how you feel.

I guess if I could teach you only one thing regarding fairness it would be this: No matter what happens to you physically in this lifetime, ultimately, if you are faithful and love God, things will work out for good.

That's not a hope or a dream. That's a promise! Paul wrote to the Christians in Rome, "And we know that all things work together for good to those who love God, to those who are called according to His purpose." There will be times in your life when you will really need to lean on this verse, as it may appear that things aren't fair. But remember, unlike your friends or your parents, God can see the big picture—and He will ultimately make everything right. He is a fair and righteous Judge (Psalm 7:11).

Something else you must consider regarding fairness is that God loves everyone (John 3:16). And because of this sincere love for His creation, we know He is not a respecter of persons. When Peter was preaching to Cornelius' household, he said, "In truth I perceive that God shows no partiality" (Acts 10:34). Remember,

Cornelius was a Gentile, and Peter was telling them that God wanted them to be saved just like the Jews. Jesus said, "For He makes His sun rise on the evil and on the good, and sends rain on the just and on the unjust" (Matthew 5:45). So while a perfect and just God created man equally—He did not create us perfect. In other words, men are not perfect. We all have sinned (Romans 3:23). Being imperfect means some of the decisions we make or with which we are forced to deal may be unfair. It means that some people may treat you unkindly or show preference to others. But this is not what God intended. God desires that we love Him and love our neighbors as ourselves (Matthew 22:37-39).

I know there may be times in which it seems the decisions your mother and I make are unfair. Understand that we, more than any other humans on the planet, love you and your soul. Our decisions, while they may seem unfair, are based on that love. There may be activities you miss or movies you don't see—because of our love for you and your soul. I promise you the easier answer would be to give in and allow you to do whatever you want. But by giving in, we have allowed Satan to win and have in essence told you: "We are not concerned where you will spend eternity." However, we do care, and as such there will be occasions that you don't get to go along with the crowd. Remember, God doesn't want us blindly following the world. He wants us to stand out (Romans 12:2).

I truly am sorry that life occasionally feels unfair. Know that all humans occasionally feel this way. But remember this doesn't change our love for you or God's love for you! Now, the real question is — how will you behave when life seems unfair?

Love

Dad

"Trust in the Lord with all your heart, And lean not on your own understanding;"
- Proverbs 3:5

It's Not all About You ... or Me

Generational names are not new. Those individuals who are now waltzing into their golden years have been long termed Baby Boomers. The X-generation watched the fall of the Berlin Wall and the end of the Cold War. The latest generation has been labeled by many as the "Me Generation." (Or maybe better termed the "I-Me" generation.) This generation has grown up embracing the notion that the world literally revolves around its very existence. Now don't get me wrong—they have had good role models. The Baby Boomers set the precedent on being a "me generation." The X-generation then filled in any missing gaps by filling their homes with gadgets, electronics, and technology to please their own desires. So now along comes an extremely narcissistic generation that expects their every want and desire to be fulfilled. Is this a healthy outlook on life, and what does the Bible have to say regarding this mentality?

Here is what I intend to teach my children—children who are currently growing up in the Me Generation:

While I love you deeply, it never has been, or never will be, all about you. That does not change my love for you, but it does help us put things into perspective. This world has existed for a long time before you and I came into it. And, Lord willing, it will continue on long after we are gone. It's not all about you. Simply put, it's all about Him.

This "I-Me" attitude has become an epidemic. During your life, you will meet many people who believe they come first—that the world truly revolves around them. Never lose sight of the fact that the Bible clearly teaches us that **every knee will bow to God** (Isaiah 45:23) no matter how rich or famous. This same sentiment is applied to Jesus in Philippians 2:9-11. How frightening will it be to look upon Jehovah God on that Great Day having lived a life revolving around yourself?

James admonished, "Humble yourselves in the sight of the Lord, and He will lift you up" (James 4:10). The Bible teaches us that one of the seven things God hates is a proud look (Proverbs 6:16-17). The inspired writer of Proverb 3:34 proclaimed that God resists the proud but gives grace to the humble. It's my prayer that you will grow into **humble** servants of God. Humility is a trait that must be cultivated in your heart. Always ask yourself why you are doing what you are doing.

No matter how great we believe our accomplishments are, there will always be someone out there who is wealthier, prettier, smarter, or more successful. There will always be someone who has traveled farther, built bigger, or accumulated more. But remember, these are worldly standards of success. If you place all of your happiness and peace in your own self-image or your own accomplishments, then you are ultimately going to live a miserable life.

In Micah 6:8 the question is raised: "And what does the Lord require of you, but to do justly, to love mercy, and to walk humbly with your God?" Is this the message we are sending today?

Having tasted every single thing this world had to offer, Solomon reminded us "Vanity of vanities, all is vanity" (Ecclesiastes 1:2). He then concluded by reminding us the whole duty of man was to "fear God and keep His commandments" (Ecclesiastes 12:13).

Please make sure this "I-Me" attitude does not infect your heart. Make sure this narcissistic attitude does not enter the Church. Our worship to God is not all about you or your personal desires. It's about Him. He is the audience of our worship and praise—not man. As you look for a husband or wife, as you raise your children, as you find a congregation with which to worship, remember Who the world truly revolves around. For without Him, the world would not revolve at all.

Love,

Dad

"Who can find a virtuous wife? For her worth is far above rubies."
- Proverbs 31:10

Pretty on the Inside

For three short years, things were going smoothly. God had blessed our family with two healthy boys and our floors were littered with balls, plastic dinosaur figurines, cars, trains, and castles. I truly believed I had this parenting thing under control. And then my little "princess" was born. And oh, how my life changed.

In the blink of an eye, I began to look at everything from a different perspective. Everything from clothes, television programs, dating, and even marriage was immediately placed under a more powerful microscope. (In fact, prearranged marriages are looking really good right now!) The pressure on young girls to be "pretty" has reached epic proportions in our society. Magazines, television, and movies are constantly bombarding our children with the idea of what is "beautiful." Ultra-thin models are paraded around as if they were the normal standard for beauty. This constant clamoring of external beauty has even caused many Christian parents to put too much emphasis on physical looks. As the world does its best to promote a worldly view of what is striking, as a parent I realize the importance of teaching a Biblical view of beauty.

Here is what I intend to teach my children about true beauty— even my young daughter who is already learning to be "pretty on the inside".

If you try to live up to the world's standard of beauty, you will lead a very unhappy life. There will always be someone out there who has a prettier complexion, better hair, or is younger looking. You can spend a great deal of time and energy trying to make yourself more attractive—even to the point of surgeries or botox injections. But none of these procedures, potions, or creams will make you beautiful in the eyes of God. I hope you will learn to be happy and confident in the external "shell" God has given you on this Earth. Never forget that God does not look at external appearances, and one day your current "shell" will be replaced with an incorruptible one (1 Corinthians 15:42). While the mainstream media wants you to believe otherwise, external beauty is fleeting and not important to Almighty God.

Without a doubt, you will meet many individuals who are very pretty on the outside—but some of these same individuals will be very unattractive on the inside. While we can't do much to alter our external looks, we can make sure that our "inside" is beautiful and very attractive to people. In 1 Samuel 16:7 we read: "But the Lord said to Samuel, 'Do not consider his appearance or his height, for I have rejected him. The Lord does not look at the things man looks at. Man looks at the outward appearance, but the Lord looks at the heart.'" Simply put, God wants you to be pretty on the inside.

How do we make ourselves pretty on the inside? We cultivate the fruit of the Spirit (Galatians 5:22-23) in our hearts. We develop a sincere love for people and their souls (Matthew 22:39; 28:19-20). We need to esteem others higher than ourselves (Philippians 2:3-4). We make sure that people know we are individuals who value integrity and honesty. We consider what we allow into our minds (Philippians 4:8), and always remember "For as he thinks in his heart, so is he" (Proverbs 23:7).

It's my desire that you grow into Christians whom your friends know they can trust; individuals who are respected for their stand for the Truth. I pray that you will cultivate the skill of genuinely listening to others and trying to help out when you can. I pray that you will learn to be givers instead of takers. And I hope that you will surround yourselves with individuals with whom you can learn and laugh. If you are able to accomplish some of these key ingredients, then almost everyone with whom you come into contact will identify you as a beautiful person indeed.

In Isaiah 53:2 the prophet reveals that the coming messiah "has no form or comeliness; and when we see Him, there is no beauty that we should desire Him." Yet, Jesus was the most beautiful person on the inside. Is this the beauty we are striving for?

The day will come when you begin looking for a mate. Your mother and I have been praying for that special person for many years. As you search for that special person, I pray that you will find someone who is beautiful on the inside—and someone who will help you get to Heaven. Do I want you to be attracted to his or her physical appearance? Sure—but I've been around long enough to know that those looks will one day fade. That smooth skin and beautiful hair will one day give way to wrinkles and a new shade of gray. That's the time in which you will treasure the importance of finding someone who is beautiful on the inside.

I hope that in the coming years people who meet you will stop in their tracks and say out loud or to themselves—wow, that person is striking…on the inside.

Love,

Dad

"The light of the eyes re-joices the heart, And a good report makes the bones healthy."
- Proverbs 15:30

Laughing ... Don't be Afraid to Smile

Why is it that many Christians walk around day after day exhibiting a sour facial expression? I suspect all teenagers have looked around church auditoriums and viewed pew after pew of individuals who all look as though they have been chewing on a bag of lemons. These are the same individuals whose lips sing "O Happy Day" but their body language appears as if they were performing Mozart's *Requiem* (Death Mass). How many times have visitors glanced around at friends and neighbors who identify themselves as Christians, only to be dazed by the sorrowful looks throughout a church building? And the dour looks don't necessarily improve outside of the church building.

There are people—young and old—who appear as if their very faces would crack if they were to smile when smiled at. Laughter has become an endangered species, as more and more people take themselves and their lives too seriously. What message are we really sending to the world when they look at us and see what appears to be expressions of unhappiness? Why would anyone want to learn more about, or join a group, who identifies themselves as "Christians" if they oftentimes look sad or depressed?

Here is what I intend to teach my children about smiles and laughter.

Always remember that we are to be reverent to God (Ecclesiastes 12:13; Daniel 6:26-27). The Bible says that we are to fear God and keep His commandments (Deuteronomy 10:12; Psalm

111:10). Our worship to Him must be decently and in order (1 Corinthians 14:26-40). This means when we enter an auditorium to worship that we mentally engage our minds on Him, and we do our best to please Him with our worship.

However, it does not mean we must continually frown in our worship to God. Nor does it mean Christians are not allowed to smile or laugh. Christians should be the happiest people on the planet, as we have been saved by the blood of Jesus Christ (1 John 1:7). Through a knowledge of the Truth and obedience to His Gospel we are saved from our sins (Hebrews 5:8-9). Our attitudes should reflect that joy and hope of eternity with Him. Our praises should spring forth from hearts that are filled with love for Him (Ephesians 5:19). Can you picture David writing his psalms to God with a frown on his face? That book—probably the most often quoted book in the Bible—became known as *Sepher Tehillim:* "The Book of Praises." When you sing and worship God, remember we are there to **praise** Him, and do so with the proper attitude and spirit.

I pray that you will approach life with a smile on your face. You have been given many gifts in your life (spiritual and material). Anytime you find yourself down or with a frown on your face remember to stop and count your blessings. Sure, you may have a bad day on occasion, but never forget to Whom you belong. You will find that smiles are contagious—and oftentimes can literally change someone's entire day. As you grow older and mature into adulthood you will learn there are appropriate and inappropriate times for smiles and laughter. For instance, when you throw a football in the living room and break one of your mom's special trinkets it is not a good time to smile. But don't be afraid to smile at appropriate times.

It's not a secret in our family that we love to laugh. During your infant years a great deal of time was spent watching you laugh and trying to make you laugh. Now that clean jokes and funny memories have entered the picture, the laughter continues in a new form. We have even ranked our family according to "most funniest" (I won't embarrass anyone and list the current ranking... although we all know who is ranked #1 and who is ranked #6!). Medically speaking, laughing is healthy and contagious. There have been occasions where you mom and I literally laughed so hard we cried—and then we laughed even more. We cherish those moments. I pray you have many occasions like that with your future mate. Remember, God created you with the ability to smile and laugh. So put a smile on and brighten someone's day.

Love,

Dad

"Pride goes before destruction, And a haughty spirit before a fall."
- Proverbs 16:18

Embarrassment

Sometimes people take life a little too seriously. They lose the ability to laugh and forget that all men are human. We want our cars washed, lawns manicured, clothes starched, and our conversation thoughtful. This air of perfection often lends itself to some pretty funny moments when reality collides. While few like to admit it, all humans have been subject to an embarrassing occasion—or two!

These moments can be even more horrifying through the eyes of a young person. For teenagers who are seeking acceptance by their peers, one small embarrassing moment in time can wind up resulting in years of tortuous ridiculing and cruel jokes. In fact, if not addressed properly, these moments can leave scars that last well into adulthood.

Given the nature of embarrassment, we rarely, if ever, discuss this topic from the pulpit. Even though almost every Christian has suffered from some type of embarrassment, we have either learned to hide it or not discuss it. We are good at coming across as having it all together. After all, we are "dignified" people, aren't we? And certainly we should not ever discuss such from the pulpit...or should we?

Here's what I intend on teaching my children about embarrassment.

I had really hoped no one saw me. You all were finishing up your ice cream (Wednesday night tradition!), and I had loudly proclaimed it was time to roll. With that statement still ringing in the air, I hit the exit door with great flair to head for the car. It was in that moment, with my face pressed up against the glass, that I realized I had selected the door that was still locked. I quickly tried to "save face" and slid over to the other door. But the damage was done—your mom (and probably others) was already "belly laughing" and relaying to each of you what Dad had just done. I knew I was busted, and that moment would be relived for months to come in the annals of Harrub history.

Our home life is full of funny family moments—some of which must remain secret to protect the innocent! Thankfully each of you is learning to laugh at yourself. This is a skill that I hope you will incorporate into your adult life. Understand that a part of being human means that we are apt to make mistakes, stumble, forget names, or just do something embarrassing. These humbling experiences are healthy reminders that we should never "get too big for our britches." These embarrassing moments do not affect who you are, nor do they affect your relationship to God. And even though you may never hear of it or see it, many of your Christian friends have experience similar embarrassing moments. It is a part of life.

The next time you find yourself embarrassed, allow it to be a reminder to you of the Bible's authenticity. Because the Bible was inspired by God and not created by any single individual (or group of people), it contains the "good, the bad, and the ugly." In other words, it doesn't hold back to give the appearance that everything is just fine. It paints the complaining Israelites in a negative light during the Exodus (see Exodus15:24; Numbers 11; Numbers 16:41-50, etc.). It doesn't try to hide the fact that some of them rebelled and the outcome was not pretty (Numbers 16). The Bible doesn't hold back at the Israelites' foolishness of creating and worshipping the golden calf (Exodus 32). As you read through some of the "ugly" accounts in God's Word, I hope you will realize that this is just one more way we have assurance that what we read is God-breathed.

God knows you are human and doesn't expect perfection—otherwise there would be no need for the redeeming blood of His Son (Romans 3:23)! In fact, it was because of His tremendous love for mankind (1 John 4:8) that He created us with free will (see Genesis 2:16-17; Joshua 24:15; Isaiah 7:15; John 5:39-40; 7:17; Revelation 22:17). When that free will collides with nature and your cheeks turn red, rest assured that we have all been there. Don't allow that moment to define who you are. Laugh it off, knowing that this is a part of life.

Let me also encourage you to be very mindful of how you treat others who embarrass themselves. Make sure they know you love them—even with all their warts!

(And remember that special counsel that we have shared at the dinner table: "At least they can't take away your birthday!") Never forget, God still wants you in Heaven with Him (1 Timothy 2:4)! In describing the good news of salvation, the prophet Isaiah proclaimed: "Instead of your shame you shall have double honor, and instead of confusion they shall rejoice in their portion. Therefore in their land they shall possess double; everlasting joy shall be theirs."

Finally, never be embarrassed about the Gospel of Jesus Christ! Do not forget the words of Paul: "For I am not ashamed of the Gospel of Christ, for it is the power of God to salvation for everyone who believes, for the Jew first and also for the Greek" (Romans 1:16).

Love,

Dad

"Hatred stirs up strife, But love covers all sins."
- Proverbs 10:12

Anger

Most people avoid confrontation like the plague. We don't like to "stir things up" or "make ripples on the pond." No one wants to be labeled a troublemaker, and we certainly don't want to wear the stigma of a "hot-headed" individual. As such, many times current, important problems go unmentioned or unaddressed. Far too many churches have put the "appearance" of peace ahead of problem resolution for fear that anger might raise its ugly head and cause even greater problems.

Anger normally finds its way into the church in one of two forms: (1) someone gets emotionally charged about something [usually personal] and flies off the handle making the entire congregation uncomfortable and occasionally causing splits; or (2) someone gets his feelings hurt and stews about it silently, only to later begin telling others [gossip] rather than handling it the way the Bible prescribes (Matthew 18). In either case, this way of dealing with anger is evil, and something to be avoided at all cost.

Here is what I intend to teach my children about anger.

I am not proud of the fact that your dad used to have an extremely fiery temper. I had two brothers who loved to pick on me, and they knew precisely what buttons to push to bring about anger. They would tease, and I would go grab a lead-weighted bat we had in the house and begin swinging for a grand slam. Thankfully, the bat was too heavy for me and gave my brothers plenty of opportunity to move before my swing would come around. One of the smartest things my dad ever did was have a "bat-burning" session in the backyard to help teach me some things about anger.

Many people will question my advice to you and may even suggest that I've lost my mind—but I pray that you do occasionally feel anger. I firmly believe that one of the reasons the church is in its current state is that too many people have become apathetic and don't get upset toward anything. In the letters to the seven churches of Asia, Jesus strongly rebuked the Christians in Laodicea for being "lukewarm" saying, "So then, because you are lukewarm, and neither cold nor hot, I will vomit you out of My mouth" (Revelation 3:16). I hope you will always be zealous and stand up for the Truth! It should anger you if the Truth is not being taught in the New Testament church!

One of the things you need to learn as you mature is how to channel that energy for good. Anger, in and of itself, is not a sin. It is what you do as a result of the anger that truly tells the story. In writing to the Christians in Ephesus, Paul warned, "'Be angry, and do not sin': do not let the sun go down on your wrath" (Ephesians 4:26). Many people allow anger to eat at them for days or years and it begins to affect their physical health as their blood pressure rises. It can also affect your mental health and cause you inner turmoil. Heed Paul's words.

There is a little known verse that many do not know that speaks of Jesus being angry. In Mark 3:5 we read, "And when He had looked around at them with anger, being grieved by the hardness of their hearts…." While many would try to explain this away and suggest Jesus wasn't actually "angry," it is wise to notice that Jesus was looking into the hearts of the Pharisees and was angry with the sin.

The key is to be angry at sin and not the sinner!

Jesus provided another example when He entered the temple and flipped the tables of the money changers (see Matthew 21:12-27; Mark 11:15-33; Luke 19:45-20:8 and John 2:12-25). Jesus wasn't going to let sin abound. We also have numerous examples of the anger of God being roused by disobedience (Uzzah in 2 Samuel 6:7; Numbers 32:10-13). Rest assured anger itself is not wrong. It is what you do in that state of mind that you must guard against.

One key is learning to be slow to anger (Proverbs 16:32; Proverbs 19:11). A fiery temper will get you into lots of trouble—trust me, I speak from past experience. We should always strive for peace (Matthew 5:9) and remember a soft answer turns away wrath (Proverbs 15:1). This one may take some practice and may be something you work on for years. But I know that one day you will be able to harness your anger for good.

Love,

Dad

"A wise son heeds his father's instruction, But a scoffer does not listen to rebuke."
- Proverbs 13:1

Enemies

The word *enemy* holds many different definitions for many different people. For some, it represents the person who cut them off on the commute into work, or maybe it's the airline industry that lost your luggage…again. For others the word has a more personal tone and represents an individual who may have been a past friend, coworker, or even family member. I suspect every adult alive has felt his/her blood pressure rise at simply the thought of some "enemy," whether it is a person with whom he/she crosses paths on a regular basis or maybe it's a terrorist on foreign soil whom he/she has never seen. Oftentimes conversations flare up and emotions run high when we hear the name of our "enemy." Our natural human inclination is to defend ourselves and paint our enemy in a negative light. Rare is the prayer that mentions our enemies, and rarer still is the sermon preached about them. Something that is powerful enough to cause our blood pressure to rise or change our mood for the entire day should not go unaddressed—especially given that God's Word speaks clearly about this subject.

Here is what I intend to teach my children about enemies.

There are some topics that are extremely easy for me to discuss with you and teach you. This is not one of those cases for me personally. I had to physically stop and pray before writing this, as this is something with which your dad struggles, and something that even today I need God to help me overcome. When people hurt us (whether it's physically or emotionally), the natural reaction is to not like those people, and oftentimes we want to strike back. However, that's not God's answer.

Heart of the Matter

I wish I could wrap you in a protective ball and tell you that everyone you meet will be friendly, and that your future coworkers will always treat you kindly. However, that is not the case. The Bible tells us that we will have enemies (Matthew 5:44; 2 Timothy 3:12). In fact, if we are living true Christian lives, we will be enemies of the world (see James 4:4; 1 John 2:15-17). Jesus said, "And you will be hated by all for My name's sake. But he who endures to the end will be saved" (Matthew 10:22). The fact of the matter is that during our lifetime we will come across people who don't like us or who act mean-spirited toward us.

Let me first remind you that you are not alone in feeling hurt or rejected. Jesus—a man Who was sinless—also had enemies. While there are many examples in the Bible of individuals who did not like Jesus or His teaching, consider that the fact that men wanted to stone Him (John 8:59). [Also look at Mark 14:1-2, Matthew 12:14, Matthew 22:15-45.] And yet, even though Jesus had the power to really dish it out to His enemies, He "killed them with kindness." As we think about our own enemies, consider where we would be today if Jesus Christ acted out against His enemies instead of going to the cross. He died for His enemies (Romans 5:8)! Don't forget that having endured a horrific scourging, beating, and the crucifixion, Jesus looked down and said, "Father, forgive them, for they do not know what they do" (Luke 23:34). Jesus Christ provided an excellent example of how to treat our enemies. Always remember what He said in the Sermon on the Mount in Matthew 5:10-12.

Understand that we are called to love our enemies (Luke 6:27, 35). While that concept may seem difficult at times, remember we can do all things through Christ Who strengthens us (Philippians 4:13). One way to help us cultivate that love is to pray for our enemies (Matthew 5:44). As you mature, you will discover it is extremely hard to carry a grudge against someone for whom you are routinely praying. Also remember that your enemies cannot separate you from God unless **you** allow them to do so (Romans 8:35-39). Finally, try hard to heap coals on their heads by following Paul's advice in Romans 12:19-21. It will take some practice, and it may be a struggle at times. But you will sleep better and enjoy life more richly when you love your enemies and remember that they too have precious souls that need to go to Heaven. [Keep this one handy, as you may need it frequently as you walk your daily walk.]

Love,

Dad

"Happy is the man who is always reverent, But he who hardens his heart will fall into calamity."
- Proverbs 28:14

Color Blind

It is refreshing and a blessing that young children are color blind. Spend a few minutes at a local park and watch small children playing together—they don't notice skin color. Children are quick to accept and quick to identify their new playmate as a "friend," but slow to notice color. Sadly, by age 7-10, children begin to notice, as witnessed by changes in behavior. Whether this perception is initiated from parents or other children is not clear, but these "differences" are sometimes translated into how they treat one another.

This difference often becomes more noticeable in adults—sometimes even within the church. Sadly, some congregations remain deliberately segregated. While we preach about diversity and everyone having a special role in the body of Christ, we may not always promote or celebrate diversity—because for many it is not comfortable. It would be a shame if pulpits herald messages about loving all people, while dark hallways echo the sounds of racial slurs and jokes. It is possible for Christians to use terms like "brothers and sisters in the faith" while treating individuals of different color like "step-families."

Teens will see this dichotomy if they hear people promoting equality while they witness deliberate segregation in the church. They will listen and know that the words of Christians don't necessarily match their actions. Perhaps through the years many congregations have been mentally labeled "hypocrites" by teens who find this behavior repugnant.

Here is what I intend to teach my children about skin color

and racism.

There is no question that the Bible teaches there is only one race—the human race. God created mankind in His image and in His likeness (Genesis 1:26-27). Humans were the pinnacle of His creative activities. The Bible clearly states that the lineage of all humanity came through one woman, Eve. She is defined as the "mother of all living" (Genesis 3:20). Never forget that we are all related—going back first to Noah and his family (Genesis 7:7,13; 1 Peter 3:20), and ultimately to Adam and Eve (Genesis 2).

Whatever the color of someone's skin, remember that he has a soul that is precious to God. Never forget that God desires all men to be saved (1 Timothy 2:4). During your life you will hear individuals—even Christians—begin conversations by saying, "I'm not racist, but…" But what?! Paul declared, "There is neither Jew nor Greek, there is neither slave nor free, there is neither male nor female; for you are all one in Christ Jesus. And if you are Christ's, then you are Abraham's seed, and heirs according to the promise" (Galatians 3:28-29).

When David—one of your favorite Biblical heroes—was about to be anointed the next king, we learned in reference to his brother, "Do not look at his appearance or at his physical stature, because I have refused him. For the Lord does not see as man sees; for man looks at the outward appearance, but the Lord looks at the heart'" (1 Samuel 16:7). I pray that you will do likewise and look inward instead of outward.

There may be times you hear Christians whom you admire of one color or another utter hateful generalizations against people of a different color. I encourage you not to give ear to this kind of talk. One wonders if these individuals secretly believe (or hope) that there will be a Heaven for each individual race? Never forget Christ is the Savior of all people—no matter what their skin looks like. Do what you can to bridge mankind together. Don't allow the hypocrisy of others to turn you away from your Creator. I pray that you will teach your children that there really is only one race. While you don't remember it today, there were many nights that you were rocked to sleep with your mom or me singing, "Jesus loves the little children, All the children of the world, red and yellow, black and white, they are precious in His sight. Jesus loves the little children of the world." Live it and pass it on.

Love,

"Hear, my children, the instruction of a father, And give attention to know understanding;"
- Proverbs 4:1

Protect Your Heart - Biblical Purity

It can come in the form of a song, the name of a city, or a neighborhood. It can even sprout from a particular food, restaurant, or the smell of familiar perfume. Having given your heart to a high school sweetheart, those memories of young love come crashing back in a single instant without a moment's notice. And sadly, the memory they bring is a reminder that our husband or wife is not the only person who has possessed a portion of our hearts.

In the Church, we occasionally teach on the importance of abstinence before marriage. We wrongly assume that by avoiding sexual relations before marriage we have completely obeyed God's will regarding dating and relationships. However, that's only part of the equation. We often neglect the importance of guarding our hearts and remaining pure.

There is an enormous difference in Biblical purity versus technical virginity—one that is rarely taught or spoken about.

Many parents view it a "success" if their children are not caught "in bed" with someone before marriage. We think nothing of our children dating dozens of individuals, as long as they can walk down the aisle a "technical virgin" on their wedding day (or given today's standard, at least without a baby on the way). But do we ever really teach our children how or why they should guard their hearts?

Here is what I intend to teach my children about protecting their hearts.

Heart of the Matter

Hopefully, by now you've learned that I am a big proponent of not blaming your parents for every "issue" with which you will struggle, when you are older (remember this when you are out of our house!). At some point you must "rise above your raising." Having said that, there is an area in which I wish my parents had been more diligent (read that "meaner") during my teenage years. I hope to do a better job in this area with you as you mature and start looking for a mate.

My parents were like the vast majority of parents during the 1980-90s. They allowed me to date young ladies and thought nothing of me having a different girlfriend every few months. As I grew older, I would date the same person for months or even years—going to restaurants, watching movies, taking hikes, going fishing, playing tennis, or just watching television. All of this seemed rather innocent and harmless—and for the most part it was. But no one warned me of the by-product of that behavior. That by-product was that I had given small pieces of my heart to many different people on many different occasions.

Your mom and I celebrated our 16-year wedding anniversary this year. I can honestly say that she is more beautiful to me today than the day we stood before God and both said, "I do!" She is an incredible woman for whom I will always be thankful. She is a model Christian wife and a spectacular mother. And that's why it hurts a little knowing she will never completely have my entire heart. Oh, physically speaking she is the **only** one for me. I have been faithful to your mother every single day since we said our vows. But those memories from past dating experiences linger. It's not that I'm interested in these other individuals—because your mom completes me. It's is just that the one gift that I wish I could give your mother—my entire heart—I'll never be able to. I wish I could simply flip a switch and completely erase the past from the old neuronal hard-drive. But the fact of the matter is, I can't.

We don't speak of this often in the Church because past memories leave a bitter taste in our mouths. The Bible speaks clearly on the importance of guarding your heart. Solomon shared his wisdom noting, "Keep your heart with all diligence, for out of it spring the issues of life" (Proverbs 4:23). Notice this is in the form of a commandment, and rightly so, as the heart is under attack (see Jeremiah 17:9-10; Matthew 15:19). Do not rush into a relationship just because it is new and exciting. Solomon wrote, "I charge you, O daughters of Jerusalem, by the gazelles or by the does of the field, **do not stir up nor awaken love until it pleases**" (Song of Solomon 2:7; see also 8:4).

Guard your heart and do not be quick to give it away. Consider the long-term consequences of giving even a small portion to someone who will eventually fade out of your life. Just because others around you are quick to "date" or "go with" someone of the opposite sex, hold yourself to a higher—more Biblical—standard.

The modern dating scene in America is not a healthy environment in which one can guard his heart. I would argue instead that it is "divorce practice," as young people give their hearts away only to later dispose of that relationship for someone else. Not many adults will openly admit to you the sorrow of not guarding your heart—but I pray you learn from my folly (Proverbs 4:1 and Proverbs 13:1). God has a beautiful plan for man and woman to be married for life (Genesis 2:24; Matthew 19:5-6). Strive to remain pure for your future mate so that one day you can give that future spouse your entire heart when you say, "I do."

Love,

Dad

"Keep your heart with
all diligence, For out of it
spring the issues of life."
- Proverbs 4:23

Dating

It happened once again. A young teenage couple in our congregation "broke up." After spending months together, sending thousands of texts back and forth, and declaring their "love" for one another, they are now picking up the pieces. Their relationship is over, resulting in emotional (and maybe physical) broken ties that will take a long time to mend. One is left wondering how many times this young lady and young man will give themselves away—emotionally and physically—before they finally walk down the aisle to marry an altogether different person?

I believe that even within the church our thinking has become poisoned in this arena. Dating has become such a major part of our culture that very few Christians even stop to consider what dating really entails. Dating holds such a "majority view" in our society that for many, this hot-button topic is not even up for discussion. Sadly, most parents have assumed a "we did it, so it must be ok" stance. As such, many homes focus on that magical age when a teen is finally able to go out on a date. Older Christians oftentimes don't help the situation—as they are often questioning young people about who they like, further promoting this boyfriend/girlfriend mindset. After all, isn't that what we do?

While it may be what the majority do, one should step back and ask if dating in modern times is a wise thing for Christian young people?

Here is what I intend to teach my children about dating.

Because my advice runs counter to our current culture, many Christians will take exception to my counsel to you. In fact, some may take personal offense. My effort here is not to offend but rather to encourage a paradigm shift on how we envision finding a future spouse. A large number of Christians have adopted a worldly perspective on finding a mate—never giving any consideration to God's Word or God's will in this matter. To the extent that the Bible addresses "premarital" relationships at all, it uses the language of men marrying and women being given in marriage (see Matthew 24:38; Luke 20:34-35). Some would argue that this was the cultural norm in the past, and that things have changed today. Since when have God's people ever taken their cues from society? Have we forgotten that we are not to be conformed to the world (Romans 12:1-12)? While there are some success stories of dating, modern dating (even modern "Christian" dating) has, in many cases, become a means for sexual activity—outside of marriage.

Dating begins with a male or female initiating a more-than-friends relationship. "Dates" are normally conducted in private, or maybe with a small group of friends, and may or may not have marriage as its end goal. I believe honest evaluation recognizes that modern dating promotes lust and provides a doorway for fornication. Consider what happens when someone creates a strong endorphin bond with a girlfriend, and then they break up years later. What is the response ten years later when that young man is married to someone else and happens to see his "old flame" in the mall? Could it not be truthfully said that in many cases dating develops an appetite for variety, promoting dissatisfaction within a future permanent bond of marriage? Additionally, modern dating develops a very self-centered "feeling" oriented version of love. Can Christian parents look at these attributes and feel comfortable that our current dating system is Biblically preparing young men and women for marriage?

In an ironic twist of fate, in the modern dating model, the father, who is supposed to be helping ensure the purity of his children, is the least involved. Rather than protecting their purity, in many cases he is the one sending them out, as hormones race through the teens' bloodstream. Sadly, the first time many fathers really meet the "boyfriend" is when he asks for the daughter's hand in marriage. My question would be for what is he really asking? He's already got what he wants! He's already stolen the daughter's heart—and maybe her purity as well. That's not honorable—that's poaching.

My hope is that rather than having a worldly checklist that characterizes the ideal fantasy spouse, you will look for a godly spouse defined by Scripture. I pray you will find someone who will help you get to Heaven and someone who will help you in your walk with God. I look forward to meeting someone who not only will help you in these areas, but someone with whom you can service and honor God better together than apart!

Your mother and I would prefer that you not experience "divorce practice." We believe that dating conditions individuals to break off relationships rather than teaching commitment. It also causes many young people to isolate themselves from their friends. We have watched on many occasions where dating leads to intimacy, but not commitment, thus devaluing the true meaning of sexual relations and marriage. Our aim is to keep you honorable before God and help you remain both physically pure as well as emotionally pure. We hope that when you really do give your heart to someone that it is the person you will marry—the one who will help you get to Heaven.

Paul declared to the church at Thessalonica, "For this is the will of God, your sanctification: that you should abstain from sexual immorality; that each of you should know how to possess his own vessel in sanctification and honor, not in passion of lust, like the Gentiles who do not know God" (1 Thessalonians 4:3-5, emp. added). Because of this your mother and I are trying to identify a better system for you to find your future mate. As you begin the important process of finding a lifelong mate I hope you will keep these key Scriptures in mind:

*1 Corinthians 6:9-7:19 (a reminder to be pure, the consequences of sexual sin, and instructions for marriage)

*1 Thessalonians 4:1-8 (teaches the importance of not defrauding another in your relationships by your words or conduct)

*Song of Solomon 2:7 ("do not awaken love before it pleases" — i.e. before the proper time)

*Proverbs 6:20-7:27 (warns us to avoid sexual sin and foolish relationships)

*James 1:13-15 (reminds us of that temptation can lead to death)

*Romans 13:8-14 (reminds us of the importance of putting others first and not seeking to please ourselves)

Romans 14:1-15:7 (reminds us to value others and do what is good for their soul's)

1 Timothy 5:1-2 (Paul admonishes young men to treat single women as sisters in Christ)

Titus 2:1-8 (encourages young men and women to focus on self-control/godliness)

John 14:15 (true love to Christ is demonstrated by obeying His commands)

My children finding your spouse is an exciting and important step—as such, we don't want you to misstep. While your mom and I have not worked out all of the "kinks," we believe court-ship is a much better model for Christians today. We will save the principles of courtship for another day. Keep studying, and keep praying for your future mate.

Love,

Dad

"My son, hear the instruction of your father, And do not forsake the law of your mother;"
- Proverbs 1:8

Courtship

Cultural historians point to the late 1800s and early 1900s as the introduction of "dating" in America. Prior to this, courtship was the normal practice. (There were even still remnants of prearranged marriage—rooted in European culture—in some pockets of America.) Dating during this time was not a separate and distinct custom, but rather it was an "evolution" of courtship practices. Prior to modern dating, young men would come to a young lady's home—and under the watchful eye of parents (and maybe siblings), a young couple would get to know one another with the intent of getting married. Dating pulled this system out of the young lady's home, away from the watchful eyes of the parents, and multiplied the number of suitors significantly.

Sadly, during this transition from courtship to modern dating the church remained quiet—taking the position that dating was a private matter. But that silence came at a very high cost. Mix into that silence the sexual revolution of the 1960s and 1970s, and one can quickly identify the recipe for disaster. It was during those silent years that millions of Baby Boomers were sexually active before marriage. They dated around and then finally settled down and got married. However, many of those marriages did not work and sadly ended in divorce.

The knee-jerk reaction from the church was to flood our teen classes with material on marriage, abstinence, and dating. The pendulum had already swung so far away from courtship that most congregations never even gave it any thought. Thankfully, many congregations are now waking up realizing that the old way of doing things is not working. As such, some parents and congregations are reanalyzing the notion of courtship.

Here is what I intend to teach my children about courtship.

First and foremost, I want you to know that your mom and I desire that you marry someone who will help you get to Heaven. This is the second biggest decision that you will make during your lifetime (the first being the decision to become a Christian). The Bible doesn't give specific commands regarding finding your mate, and as such Christians must look at Biblical precepts and use common sense. While we don't believe in "arranged marriages" (even though it is awfully tempting!), we do want to help and guide you through the selection process. In Colossians 3:17 we read, "And whatever you do in word or deed, do all in the name of the Lord Jesus, giving thanks to God the Father through Him." This includes selecting a mate.

It does not make any sense for us to watch over your souls in every other aspect of your life, but then send you out by yourself and "hope you find a good one."

As I've said many times, "hope" is not a strategy for success.

Merriam Webster defines courting as engaging "in social activities leading to engagement and marriage." It entails a single man going through the father of a single young lady. Notice that it has marriage as its end goal. **Courtship entails a different motive than dating**—the motive is to find a spouse.

If marriage is the end goal, then we should ask why anyone would get involved in a relationship with someone if they were not candidates for marriage? For young men this means they have secured a job that will allow them to provide for himself and his future spouse.

Courtship also entails a different mindset. Rather than looking for someone based solely on external features, having a checklist of qualities you desire, and judging how someone makes you "feel," you search for a godly spouse. This needs to be someone you can love, and yes are attracted to, but more importantly, someone who will help you serve the Lord and will help you get to Heaven. Abraham loved his son so much he sent his servant back to his home country to find a wife (Genesis 24). Notice that Rebekah agreed to be married to Isaac having never seen him. Likewise, Isaac had never seen Rebekah prior to the day he was walking in the field.

Finally, **courtship entails a different method**. In courtship the young man goes through the father—who vets the young man as a possible suitor. The father approaches the daughter to discern if this is someone in whom she has an interest. And then after clearance is given, the young couple use group/public situations to get to know each other and their families. While there is not a "paint-by-numbers" detailed method, the process is one that everyone feels will protect the heart and purity of both individuals.

Please understand that your mom and I don't have all the answers in this area—and there will be some trial and error. But we are committed to helping you walk down the aisle honorable before God and finding someone who loves your soul as much as we do. We continue to pray for that person.

Love,

"Let your fountain be blessed, And rejoice with the wife of your youth. As a loving deer and a graceful doe, Let her breasts satisfy you at all times; And always be enraptured with her love."
- Proverbs 5:18-19

Marriage Takes 3

It used to be uncommon and unspoken. However, today divorce has reached epidemic proportions. According to the U.S. Census Bureau, the ratio of marriages to divorces is 2 to 1. While a husband and wife may vow to love one another in sickness and in health, for richer and poorer, and for better and worse, the reality is that many individuals only stick around during times of wealth, health, and happiness. Many people can remember years ago when parents in America would often have many children. Today children oftentimes have many parents. Sadly, the concept of commitment has been lost in our "disposable" and "instant gratification" world. There is no doubt that the tentacles of divorce reach deeply inside most—if not all—church families. And those tentacles have caused many problems throughout the body of Christ. While we don't talk about it much for fear we may offend some, this topic desperately needs to be addressed in order to stem the epidemic.

Here is what I intend to teach my children about divorce.

A good marriage is one of the richest blessings you will ever know. It is an institution that was formed by God (Genesis 2:22-24). While we pray that you are able to experience it one day, we want each one of you to realize that you do not have to be married or be a parent to serve God faithfully. Consider for a moment all of the Biblical examples of faithful individuals who were single or barren/childless (e.g., Paul, Dorcas, King David's wife Michal).

Believe it or not, your mother and I have been praying for you and your future spouses (and even their parents!) since before you were born. This topic is so crucial that we believe the time to start teaching you the importance of marriage and relationships is not when you are a teenager, but rather from your toddler years on up. Aside from your decision to be a Christian and your relationship with God, there is nothing more important on this planet. This special person will either help or hinder your journey to Heaven. **Our prayer is that your mate will be a strong Christian who can help you in your spiritual journey.** We hope that as you grow and mature you will select someone with whom to spend your life who has similar values and priorities.

Make no mistake about it good marriages take a great deal of work. You won't receive a "how-to" book along with your marriage certificate. This is one reason it is so important to keep your marriage God-centered. The relationship you see daily between your mom and me did not happen overnight. We have been together through good years and bad. We have had to learn how to communicate effectively with one another, how to fight fair, how to compromise, and how to let our words be reflected in our actions. With each happy memory and each trial, our relationship has deepened and grown. However, even after being married as long as we have, we still have to invest time and energy into our marriage. That is why we try to regularly have "date night" without any children present—to reconnect, rekindle, and grow our own relationship.

Your mother and I have a rule that divorce "is not even an option." We made this pledge to one another very early in our marriage, and it has been comforting during times of trial. The Bible is clear that **God hates divorce** (Malachi 2:16). Never forget that God joins you together with your mate (Matthew 19:6), and His original intention was that man and woman remain married until death (Mark 10:2-9). Study carefully Matthew 19:8, where Jesus explains that while divorces were permitted because of the hardness of their hearts, but "from the beginning it was not so."

Keep your marriage intact and avoid divorce! Invest time and energy in one another. If you feel things are spiraling out of control talk to your parents, preacher, elders, or godly friends. (Don't confide problems to a friend of the opposite sex, as that can often lead to danger.) Find a happily married, faithful couple with whom you can spend time and glean wisdom. Take time to find activities that both you and your spouse enjoy, and do those. Be willing to compromise. And do your best to never take your spouse for granted. The Bible is the best source for how men are to love their wives (Ephesians 5:25) and how wives are to treat their husbands (Titus 2:4-5; Ephesians 22-23). That's a whole different topic!

In Matthew 19, Jesus outlines the **only** allowance for divorce and remarriage—sexual immorality (verse 9). That's it. Divorce and remarriage is not allowed simply for irreconcilable differences or because one party is no longer happy. Many people have tried to manipulate this passage to find exceptions or make loopholes. In fact, many men with advanced degrees have desperately tried to argue that they possess a "newfound wisdom" about what this Scripture actually means. But as we have taught you from childhood, you don't need advanced degrees to understand the important matters of the Bible. God is able to effectively communicate His plan on marriage and divorce.

Never change your views on Biblical matters simply because it has become personal. Remember, God is immutable (Malachi 3:6)— He and His Word do not change. It is usually the case that those trying to conjure up "exceptions" to Jesus' teaching on marriage have personal stakes involved. For instance, maybe their children, other relatives, or friends have divorced for reasons other than sexual immorality, and they want to find a way for them to remarry. But the Scriptures are clear.

Many try to offer excuses to justify divorce and remarriage such as, "One party was not baptized at the point of marriage," or "Children are involved," or "The original intent was not for a Biblical permanent marriage." They use mental gymnastics to find loopholes between Matthew 19 and 1 Corinthians 7:10-13. Remember, these commands were written to believers and unbelievers, thus baptism does not alter an adulterous marriage. Notice that 1 Corinthians 7:10 clearly states: "Now to the married I command, yet not I but the Lord: A wife is not to depart from her husband. But even if she does depart, let her remain unmarried or be reconciled to her husband. And a husband is not to divorce his wife." The decision to marry is important and should not be entered into lightly or because of temporal lust. Your mom and I agree that rather than jumping through hoops and rearranging the original intent looking for a "way out" years later, your time would be better invested in creating and building a healthy marriage that includes God.

This is why trust is so vital in a marriage.

Go the extra mile and give your spouse information as to where you will be—don't leave them wondering. Post a copy of your wedding picture or vows to your computer. Keep that golden band on your finger as a constant reminder.

On the day your mom and I said our wedding vows, the man who baptized me read a poem that I want to share. It's titled "Marriage Still Takes Three" (author unknown). I look forward to reading it at your wedding one day in the future.

I once thought marriage took
Just two to make a go,
But now I am convinced
It takes the Lord also.

And not one marriage fails
Where Christ is asked to enter,
As lovers come together
With Jesus at the center.

But marriage seldom thrives,
And homes are incomplete,
Till He is welcomed there
To help avoid defeat.

In homes where Christ is first,
It's obvious to see,
Those unions really work,
For marriage still takes three.

Love,

Dad

P.S. While you may not welcome the idea, your mom and I really like the idea of "prearranged marriages," so we are happily accepting applications from faithful parents of children your ages!

"*A wise son makes a glad father; But a foolish son is the grief of his mother.*"
- Proverbs 10:1

Headship

I was not yet born when the second wave of feminism rocked the United States in the 1960s. Subsequent waves have campaigned for gender equality in every aspect of life. The office environment has changed as women join men climbing the corporate ladder. Homes have changed as roles and responsibilities shifted. And even some churches have embraced gender equality as they welcomed women preachers into pulpits or elected women elders to watch over the flock. We even now have a "gender-neutral" Bible in which God is not viewed in a masculine but rather in a neutral gender. The media does a phenomenal job of keeping these matters in the forefront of everyone's mind—for fear that any abatement would result in women being relegated to an inferior status.

The one place that feminism has unleashed the most damage is between married couples. The concept of "headship" is viewed as radical and barbaric. Our children are learning the notion of gender equality in many classrooms at a very young age. Anyone even suggesting the idea that a man should be "over" a woman is broadly painted as dictatorial, abusive, and living in the Dark Ages. Because of this intimidation from the media, textbooks, and activist groups, the notion of headship has sometimes fallen silent in the church. We try to straddle the fence and not offend anyone.

Here is what I intend to teach my children about headship.

From a very young age, you all have argued about who gets to "go first," who gets to "ride shotgun," who gets to be "king" of the fort, and who gets to play with certain toys. Some of you argue your age or position in the family in an effort to get your way. My (only) daughter often plays the "but I'm a girl" card as she bats her long eyelashes. This constant battle has brought on many family devotionals about Jesus' words regarding "the last will be first, and the first last" (Matthew 20:16). We pray that as you grow you will strive to be a servant for Him.

As you mature into adulthood and put away the toys, we want you to develop a proper attitude toward your God-given role and responsibility. I have seen far too many homes where the marriage roles do not model Christ and the church, which cause all kinds of problems. Remember that only men and women were created in the image and likeness of God. The animals were simply formed from the ground by God (Genesis 2). As such, mankind holds a special place in the eyes of God. While we were both made in the image and likeness of God, men and women have special and unique roles. The glory of man was that woman was created for him. The glory of woman was that man was incomplete without her. I believe it is critical to you and your marriages to learn more about your roles.

Early in man's history, in the opening chapters of Genesis, we find the concept of male headship first being formed. In His infinite wisdom God recognized it was not good for man to be alone (Genesis 2:18). After Adam named all of the animals, there was still not a helpmeet suitable for Adam (Genesis 2:20). Thus God formed a woman from the rib of Adam. Her role was to be a helper to Adam as they both served the Lord. Do not miss the point that God brought woman to the man (Genesis 2:22) instead of bringing the man to woman. She was to help in every aspect of his life—physical, emotional, spiritual, mental, sexual, and social. Just a few verses later, when God is delivering judgment on the sin in the Garden of Eden, He tells the woman, "In pain you shall bring forth children; your desire shall be for your husband, and he shall rule over you" (Genesis 3:16). Notice that woman was made for man, from man, and that she was made later than the man. Man was to work and keep the garden, while the woman acted as his helper. As such, you should not be afraid to rear your own little boys to be masculine and rear your daughters to be feminine. These roles were set out from the beginning. None of this is to suggest that she is inferior to man, but rather it is to demonstrate our God-given positions.

I know that this concept of male headship causes lots of anger and emotion in many people. (In fact, I will probably receive some negative letters because of my words.) Some will argue that the roles were only pertinent to Old Testament times or that the concept of headship was a cultural issue. These same individuals are quick to quote passages like Galatians 3:28, "There is neither Jew nor Greek, there is neither slave nor free, there is neither male nor female; for you are all one in Christ Jesus." However, a quick examination of the text reveals the weakness of these arguments. If God no longer intends for man to rule over the woman (Genesis 3:16), then why do women still experience pain in childbirth today? Second, were Paul's words literal regarding mankind losing all of their distinctions—meaning could someone shed his cultural heritage of being a Jew or Greek, or his language? Absolutely not. He was trying to convey that we are equal in Christ. The blood of Jesus Christ flowed equally for men and women.

Lest you think headship applies only in the Old Testament, consider Paul's admonition to the church at Ephesus. He declared, "Wives, submit to your own husbands, as to the Lord. For the husband is the head of the wife, as also Christ is head of the church; and He is the Savior of the body. Therefore, just as the church is subject to Christ, so let the wives be to their own husbands in everything" (Ephesians 5:22-24). Other skeptics will point to the verse just prior to this that says, "Giving thanks always for all things to God the Father in the name of our Lord

Jesus Christ, submitting to one another in the fear of God" (Ephesians 5:20-21). But if we are only to submit to one another, how then do we harmonize the instructions given in Titus 2 that "older women likewise, that they be reverent in behavior, not slanderers, not given to much wine, teachers of good things—that they admonish young women to love their husbands, to love their children, to be discreet, chaste, homemakers, good, obedient to their own husbands, that the word of God may not be blasphemed" (Titus 2:3-5; see also admonitions regarding submission in 1 Corinthians 11; 1 Timothy 2).

Now before my boys get this grand notion that they are going to be "king" and "rule the roost," I want to remind you that part of being head also means being a greater servant and example. Don't think of it as a position but rather a job—and a hard one at that! For you see, the passage in Ephesians continues by saying, "Husbands, love your wives, just as Christ also loved the church and gave Himself for her" (Ephesians 5:25). Being "head" is more than barking out orders. Anyone who thinks I am going to give my daughter's hand to someone who intends to rule the home with an iron fist, or be a harsh dictator, or be verbally abusive obviously does not know me. I'm looking for a true leader who will act as her head, a man who will love her as Christ loved the church. This man can lead in all aspects of life. He should be a spiritual leader, taking time to grow in the Word and ensuring the family gets to Heaven. He should be head in the example of righteousness. It's not enough to talk the talk—a true leader will walk the walk and set the pattern for the family. He should lead in intimacy keeping the marriage bed pure. He should be head in the financial well-being of the family as well.

Male headship is a fine balance. A man who overextends male headship is likely to be abusive, whereas someone who undervalues it will likely not step up to the plate and lead. I pray that my example in our home has provided a blueprint for you to follow. You recognize that in our home I consult and talk with your mother on almost everything— from little matters to major decisions. I work hard to treat your mother with respect and to let her know what a vital role she plays in our family. I try to demonstrate my love for her with every fiber of my being in my role as the head of our family. I hope you will study your roles from God's Word and not allow the world to dictate what they think your roles should be.

Love,

"For the lips of an immoral woman drip honey, And her mouth is smoother than oil; But in the end she is bitter as wormwood, Sharp as a two-edged sword."
- Proverbs 5:3-4

Adultery

Adultery does not start in the bedroom. Oftentimes it starts with a lively conversation or maybe a Facebook exchange. Conversations blossom into flirting. Flirting then takes on a whole new dynamic as personal feelings are shared. Rather than sitting down with a spouse and sharing problems and concerns, individuals spill their guts to a stranger who is quick to console and provide emotional—and eventually physical—support.

I dare say there is not a congregation in the church that has not felt the devastating effects of adultery. Our hearts sink when we hear about yet another couple torn apart by the tentacles of infidelity. Occasionally, the sin is committed with someone outside the church family. Many times, however, a married individual turns to someone within the church family. Multiple families are destroyed as selfish individuals seek their own pleasure and treat their marriages like a doormat. Adultery has affected young and old, rich and poor. We can all identify friends, preachers, deacons, and elders who have turned their lives upside down in search of greener grass. Few consider the lasting damage to their children, their families, the church, and their relationship with God in search of a few moments of physical pleasure. It's the heat of the moment.

Here is what I intend to teach my children about adultery.

I'm going to make an admission that will likely get me into a great deal of trouble: Your mother has more wrinkles and gray hair than the day I asked her to marry me. (I do too for that matter!) But I can honestly say that when I look at your mother today she is more beautiful than the day we married. Many times I will look at her without her knowing and smile from ear to ear at how lucky I am to be married to such a beautiful woman. Your mother has a beauty that radiates from her very soul. I found a Proverbs 31 woman and I rejoice with the wife of my youth (Proverbs 5:18). I pray that one day you will be able to experience a similar feeling.

Marriage is for life. It is the second biggest decision you will make in your lifetime. The vows you make before God, your family, and friends are not to be taken lightly. The way in which you view the opposite sex must change on that day, as you are no longer "looking" for someone. Your search is over—forever! (Matthew 5:27-30).

Your marriage should focus on getting one another to Heaven.

If you get married and focus on what you "don't" have, I assure you that your marriage will suffer. Allow me to be blunt for a moment: There will **always** be someone out there with more physical beauty, talents, or wealth than your spouse. (You are not excluded from this either!) However, always remember that just because the grass may appear greener does not mean it tastes good or doesn't come with some serious maintenance. It is easy to focus a great deal of importance on physical things when you are young, but physical things will eventually fade away. I want to encourage you to focus on the beautiful grass with which you have been blessed and count your blessings every single day.

One wonders how much Solomon knew of his dad's relationship with Bathsheba. Consider the warning he gave against adultery in Proverbs 5. After describing the immoral woman's lips as dripping honey and her mouth smoother than oil (vs. 3), he goes on to say, "Remove your way from her. And do not go near the door of her house" (vs. 8). Don't even place that temptation before you. When one combs through God's Word and researches the topic of marriage, divorce, and remarriage, the action of infidelity keeps bubbling up as a lynchpin (Matthew 19; 1 Corinthians 7) that—like death—can sever a marriage. It is a sin that was singled out in the Ten Commandments (Exodus 20:14). Guard against it with diligence!

Your mom and I occasionally talk about the reality of adultery. We are smart enough to recognize that the devil is "seeking whom he can devour" (1 Peter 5:8), and that includes the two of us! I am careful not to be alone with any woman other than your mother. I will often talk about my wife and children in front of individuals so they know I am a family man. We know if either of us let our guard down then devastating things could happen. As such, we try to be proactive to ensure that we are never in that position. From basic things like sharing computer passwords to more advanced things like phoning and letting one another know where we are, we are committed to one another (and God!).

I pray that you will "drink water from your own cistern" and work hard to make your mate happy (Proverbs 5:15-20). Read Song of Solomon with your spouse and fulfill one another's physical needs. Enjoy the intimacy of your marriage and flee temptation. Lastly, my child, never forget the things I have taught you…Proverbs 3:1-6.

Love,

"These six things the Lord hates, Yes, seven are an abomination to Him: A proud look, A lying tongue, Hands that shed innocent blood,"
- Proverbs. 6:16-17

Please, Please Don't - Abortion

Most of us know someone—even if we really do not know about "it" firsthand. It may be a high school classmate who "got into trouble" at the tender age of sixteen. Or it may be a coworker who was climbing the corporate ladder. Or it may even be the person sitting in the same pew with you on Sunday morning. Rare is the congregation in which at least one member has not had an abortion. Sometimes the secret is shared with close friends; other times, it is literally taken to the grave. Having talked to several women (and even a couple of men) who made this "choice," I realize that it is often a decision made under great stress—and a decision that can leave scars for life.

Here is what I intend to teach my children about abortion.

With the exception of Claire, I had the pleasure of watching each one of you enter this world and take your first breaths—and I only missed Claire by two hours. (And yes, I am strongly considering making her wait on me two hours before walking her down the aisle, since she just couldn't wait!) Each time we discovered we were expecting, your mother and I would quietly wonder, "Can we do this?" As our family grew, we wondered "Can we love another one as much?" The answer to both questions was a resounding "Yes!" Our love just continued to grow as our family grew. Now we cannot envision a world without each one of you. It is my prayer that you, too, will one day know the joy of being a father or mother. Our family is one of the deepest sources of happiness we know, topped only by the knowledge of our salvation through Jesus Christ.

While your mom and I have big plans for your future—including your impact and influence on His Church—we are not so naive as to think that those plans will unfold without a few hiccups and hurdles along the way. If the plans get brushed aside, please don't throw away the entire blueprint! Paul, in writing about the "plan" for younger widows, observed: "I desire that the younger widows marry, bear children, manage the house,…" I hope you will always keep that divinely laid down order in mind. We are to marry first, and then have children. However, if that plan is lost due to a moment of passion, **please come to us. Please, please don't have an abortion or consent to one.**

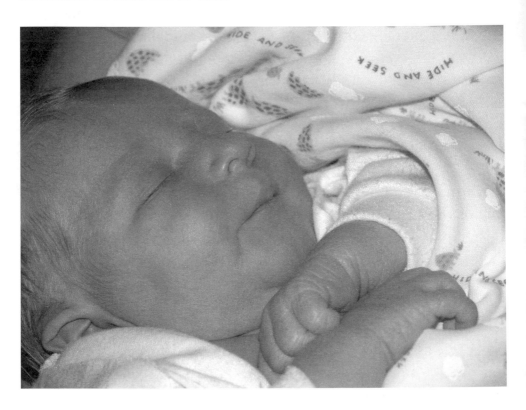

Never try to correct a mistake by making another one, and please do not counsel anyone else to do likewise. Far too many people find themselves in situations in which they are unexpectedly pregnant, and they feel the only answer is to abort the child. Without question, abortion stops a beating heart—just 18 days after conception, the baby's heart begins to beat. You do not want to spend the rest of your life with emotional scars, always thinking "What if…" I promise you that, with Christ, we can get through it, together (Philippians 4:13). Never ever forget that we love you, and you can always come to us!

Would your mom and I be humbled? Absolutely. Would it hurt? Definitely. But would we forgive you and help you turn a wrong into a right? Without question! Remember you can repent of your sins and ask for forgiveness, and God will forgive you (1 John 1:7-10). In fact, if this were to happen, I would hope that you would then one day have the courage to use your own experience to teach others.

These six things the Lord hates. Yes, seven are an abomination to Him: a proud look, a lying tongue, hands that shed innocent blood" (Proverbs 6:16-17). What is more innocent than the blood of an unborn child?

Since your birth we have tried to remind you that humans are different from the animals. We were made in the image and likeness of God (Genesis 1:26-27). Every living human has been instilled with a soul (see James 2:26; Ecclesiastes 12:7). Please do not ever consider ending a life prematurely—rather allow us to help you train up that child so that one day it can grow up to become a child of God. Think about that tiny soul lodged in that little unborn child. Abortion is an abomination to God, and I hope you never forget that.

Love,

Dad

"The mouth of the righteous brings forth wisdom, But the perverse tongue will be cut out."
- Proverbs 10:31

Cursing and Cussing

It is getting harder and harder to avoid them—cuss words. We hear them at ball games, we read them in novels, we listen to them on television (even commercials now!), and we see "friends" use them on Facebook. As our society continues to lose its moral footing, our language falls deeper and deeper in the gutter. Long gone are the days when a single word—as was uttered in Gone with the Wind—will cause the nation to pause and consider what is moral and right. Instead, we have song lyrics today that would cause many sailors to blush.

So where is the church in all of this profanity? Have we allowed our voices to be heard, or do we just turn a deaf ear. How many times have we heard that the latest blockbuster movie was "really good, except I think it had a few bad words in it." The truth reveals many Christians have become desensitized to cursing. The contagion of "potty mouth" has influenced and infected far too many Christian homes today. Add to this that many congregations continue to put on blinders as their young people type obscenities and euphemisms in the public domain of Facebook.

Here is what I intend to teach my children about cursing and cussing.

So, it's confession time. There was a time when your dad did not use wisdom in choosing his words. In fact, there was a time that I possessed a potty mouth. It bothers me to say that, but I want you to know the truth and the struggles that I endured with it. I am not proud of it, and am thankful that the blood of Christ is able to forgive the sins of my past! Never forget that once you make the poor choice of incorporating profanity into your vocabulary, it is extremely hard to weed it out. Better to never start—than to have to consciously remind yourself that Christians do not use that language. (This is why we try very hard to filter what is coming into our house!)

There are three categories of cursing/cussing. The first involves cursing God. When the Ten Commandments were handed down to the Israelites God made sure they understood He would not stand for this. "You shall not take the name of the Lord your God in vain, for the LORD will not hold him guiltless who takes His name in vain" (Exodus 20:7; see also Deuteronomy 5:11). Make no mistake about it, you are not to ever curse God or use His name in a derogatory fashion!

The second category is cursing (or swearing) someone or something. Again, the Bible is very clear that cursing is not something Christians should be doing. There is often a very negative connotation associated with individuals who curse. Consider passages like Psalm 10:7, "His mouth is full of cursing and deceit and oppression; under his tongue is trouble and iniquity." (See also Psalm 59:12; 109:17; Romans 3:13-18; James 5:12; Leviticus 19:12). Use your words very carefully, and do not get into the habit of cursing someone or something.

The third category is what we might commonly refer to as cussing or profanity. This one is a little more tricky—kind of like nailing Jell-o to a tree. There is not a specific list of words in the Bible that I can point you to and say "Do not say those." Our language changes—as does the meaning for some words. What might have been considered profane fifty years ago may no longer be a word that is used, or it may mean something different. As such, my words to you in this category are to use wisdom and consider your influence. Christians should be conscious of their speech and use it for good. Paul admonished, "Let no corrupt word proceed out of your mouth, but what is good for necessary edification, that it may impart grace to the hearers" (Ephesians 4:29; see also Proverbs 25:11). You will know what words are considered "bad words" and which are not. As Paul urged the church at Colossae "Let your speech always be with grace, seasoned with salt, that you may know how you ought to answer each one" (Colossians 4:6).

Again, in Paul's letter to the church at Colossae he reminded the Christians to put off all of these: "anger, wrath, malice, blasphemy, filthy communications out of your mouth."

I pray that as you grow and mature you will use your mouth to build up and encourage. Nowadays, when I hear people cuss I often wonder if they choose those words because they have such a poor vocabulary? As the writer of Proverbs said "The heart of the wise teaches his mouth, and adds learning to his lips" (16:23).

Love,

"Do not withhold good from those to whom it is due, When it is in the power of your hand to do so."
- Proverbs 3:27

Compliments and Conversation

Traveling the world, it has become increasingly clear that many in younger generations crave and enjoy "the spotlight." Growing up in the era of reality T.V., some in Generation Y or "Millennials" are consciously or unconsciously seeking the praises of men in an effort to fill a void in their lives. This is not new—as the Bible indicates, there have always been individuals who love the praises of men (Haman in Esther 3:5; Matthew 23:5-6; John 12:43). Unfortunately, many never learn how to properly give (or receive) praise to others. My fear is that our society has become so self-centered that sincere compliments have fallen out of style. Compliments have become tools that are only doled out when someone wants something.

Furthermore, we have become such a "sound-bite" nation that normal conversation is a thing of the past. How ironic is it that we live during an era in which technology makes global communication incredibly easy—and yet, people are losing the ability to communicate face-to-face. The younger generation is more tech savvy than any other previous generation, but that same technology is isolating them from reality. Texting and Facebooking are proving to be stumbling blocks to real communication. (How sad is it when a family of four walks into a res-taurant and everyone is so "plugged in" to phones and video games that aside from placing their orders, they don't communicate with one another at the table?) This inability to effectively communicate is a blight on our society—and will only get worse unless parents teach their children to communicate and compliment others.

Here is what I intend to teach my children about communication and compliments.

Carrying on a conversation with people is not something that can be taught in a book. Oh sure, there are books and classes on communication, but these come up short compared to the real world. It is similar to public speaking—you can take classes or get advice, but the only way to really be comfortable speaking in public is to jump in and do it over and over. Learn how to ef-fectively communicate with those around you—and look them in the eyes when you speak.

One of the greatest joys you will ever experience cannot be purchased and it doesn't cost you a thing. That joy is fellowship with like-minded souls. As boring as it may initially sound to you, sitting around a living room discussing life and "the good old days" is a pleasure that many don't experience these days. Before you all came in the picture, your mom and I would frequent-ly call friends (like the Palmers), and on the spur of the moment we would combine our dinners, staying up to the wee hours of the night just talking. I can't recall the television or radio ever be-ing on. We were just a handful of friends sitting around talking about life, our society, and reli-gion. I wouldn't trade those memories for anything.

Let me strongly encourage you to learn to take an interest in others and allow them to share their wisdom and funny tales with you. Be sincere and be honest in your conversation (Co-lossians 4:6). You will meet many individuals who are only interested in what they can get from a conversation. In fact, many words have been shared for the express intent of receiving some-thing in return. Don't follow this pattern. When you approach a conver-sation be genuine and en-ter the conversation with the hope of growing closer to the individual you are talking to. Turn off the iPod, hang up the phone, and learn to talk face-to-face.

In addition, don't be scared to compliment others or worry about what others will think. If you truly mean it, there is nothing wrong with pointing out when someone does something good or dresses nice (Proverbs 16:24). Everyone you meet during your lifetime appreciates nice words being said about him or her. Now some may not admit it, or may become slightly embar-rassed—but all humans like hearing compliments. When someone pays you a compliment, a simple "thank you" is all that is necessary. Many people learn how to give a compliment but they never learn how to accept a compliment graciously. These communication tools will be useful throughout your life. Never forget the inspired words found in Psalm 19:14.

Love,

Dad

If you enjoyed this book check out:

CONVICTED
A Scientist Examines the Evidence for Christianity

by Brad Harrub, Ph.D.

For more of his material go to www.focuspress.org